# Children of the Tower

JULIA DOBSON

# Children of the Tower

ILLUSTRATED BY
JEROO ROY

*Foreword by the Resident Governor of the Tower*

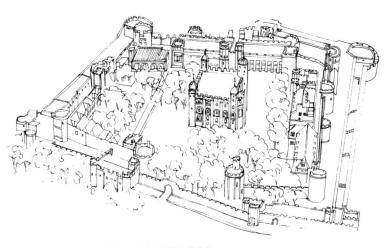

HEINEMANN : LONDON

William Heinemann Ltd
15 Queen Street, Mayfair, London W1X 8BE

LONDON MELBOURNE TORONTO
JOHANNESBURG AUCKLAND

First published 1978
Text © Julia Dobson 1978
Illustrations © William Heinemann 1978
434 93459 3

**To my father**

Printed in Great Britain by
Cox & Wyman Ltd
London, Fakenham and Reading

# Contents

# Foreword by the Resident Governor of Her Majesty's Tower of London

*I first met Julia Dobson when she visited the Tower to gather material for* Children of the Tower. *At the time I was struck with her knowledge and her scholarly approach to her subject. You may be sure that all her facts are historically accurate. The book, though, is much more than a catalogue of Tower events. The author's inventive approach and her lucid and graceful style make the book a special pleasure to read. It is written in the first place for children but, like all the best children's books, it will appeal equally to grown-ups.*

*Digby Raeburn*

# Author's Note

*In the writing of this book, I owe a debt of gratitude to Major-General W. D. Raeburn, the Resident Governor of the Tower, for his co-operation, to Peter Hammond, Education Officer of the Tower, for his unfailing patience and help, to Stephen Freer for his historical advice, and to Toby Roxburgh who read the manuscript.*

*Julia Dobson*

# The Tower through the Ages

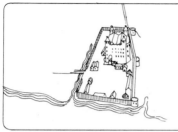

1100, at the death of William Rufus. Part of the Norman ditch on the west can still be seen, as can remains of the Roman walls on the southeast and east.

1216. King John had completed the expansion of the Tower begun in the reign of Richard I. Only the Bell Tower, then at the southwest corner, survives.

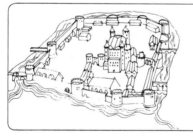

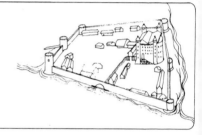

1272. Henry III had built what became the inner wall and towers (the Wakefield Tower is the largest and least changed of these) and the palace south of the White Tower.

1307. Edward I had extended the Tower to its present size. He made the moat and built two well-defended entrances, by land in the southwest (of this the Middle and Byward Towers remain) and on the river, at the watergate later called Traitors' Gate.

1547. Henry VIII had repaired the medieval defences, added to the palace, and built St Peter's Chapel and the Queen's House on Tower Green.

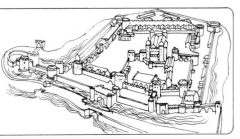

The Tower today. Most of the castle buildings remain in some form. The palace has gone. So have the buildings of the Mint and Menagerie and all but one of the Ordnance storehouses. Nowadays building is allowed only on a small scale and in keeping with the Tower's historic character.

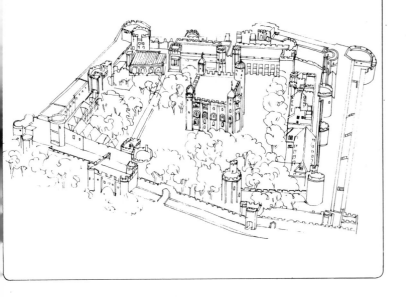

# Prologue:
# How the Tower was Built

THE TOWER OF LONDON was built by William the Conqueror. The site chosen for it was an obvious one. It was built on the foundations of several Roman buildings in the south-east corner of the surviving Roman wall round the city. There was already a temporary castle on the site, made of timber and earth, which had been hastily erected by the Conqueror after his army had occupied London, and he had been crowned in Westminster Abbey.

To make way for the new tower, the old one was demolished, and building materials were brought to the site. Timber was dragged in by oxen. Blocks of Caen limestone from Normandy were unloaded from boats at the quayside. Mudstone was dredged up from the river, and ragstone from Kent came in barges down the Medway. The site became cluttered with poles for scaffolding, ladders, pulleys, baskets, axes, chisels and saws.

Wooden shacks sprang up all over the place to house groups of craftsmen such as blacksmiths and carpenters, who considered themselves superior to the bulk of the labour force. A master mason was in control of the day-to-day details of the building. He was the man who organized the labour force and checked the work as it progressed. He earned around twelve shillings a week—a princely sum in comparison with a stonemason, who earned two or three pence a day. But there was someone more important than the master mason who was in overall control. This was the churchman Gundulf. He had formerly been a monk in the famous abbey of Bec and had come to England some years after the Conquest. In 1076 King William made him Bishop of Rochester and in 1078 put him in charge of the Tower of London.

Gundulf had been involved in the building of stone castles and churches in Normandy, and he was an able administrator. He did not spend all his time in London, for he was a busy man and had other commitments, but from time to time he would come to the site to see how the work was proceeding. He would be accompanied by a clerk who carried his plans on a wooden board, and a translator who made the Bishop's French instructions plain to the English-speaking craftsmen and labourers.

After the ground plan was staked out, work began in earnest, and the labourers started digging deep foundation trenches through the clay. When the firmer gravel was reached, digging stopped, and shells and Roman bricks and bits of tiles were crammed into the bottom of the trenches. Upon this base the foundation stones were laid. The walls were made of rough pieces of stone, set in mortar mixed from lime and sand by the labourers. More regularly-shaped pieces of rubble were chosen for the outside surfaces and set into courses so as to give a smoother appearance to the walls. The walls were supported by wooden frames until the mortar had set. Cut stones were used for corners and openings and the plinth.

From Easter to Michaelmas (29 September) the workers on the site made use of every daylight hour. Summoned by a rising bell at dawn, they would dress in their woollen drawers, knee-length shirts and leg bandages and work until midday when they would break off for a rest and a simple meal of bread and pottage. Then they would work until the last bell of the day bade them lay down their tools. Sundays and Holy Days were rest days when men and boys would desert the site to go walking in Smoothfields, or rabbiting in St John's Wood.

After Michaelmas, the working day became shorter and shorter and many labourers were laid off to survive the winter as best they could. At Easter, work returned to normal and the site became alive again. It was not only the labourers who returned, but all the familiar hangers-on, the farmers, the trades people, the washerwomen and all the others who serviced the everyday needs of the site, as well as prostitutes, strolling players, and fortune-tellers.

One year followed another. People were born and died. There were delays, disasters, and diseases, but little by little the Tower grew until there came a time, some years after the Conqueror had died, when the disgruntled Londoners found themselves looking up at a massive fortress. It dwarfed the Roman wall; it towered over the hovels, the timber and plaster houses, and the stone buildings in their own defensive walls or burgs; it topped the church spires, even St Paul's; it commanded a view of the outlying villages, and it scanned the river to the west and to the east.

From a defensive viewpoint the castle looked formidable. Around the tower were the outer defences, consisting of the two sections of Roman wall linked by a timber stockade on top of an earth rampart with a ditch in front. In 1097 the earth and timber section was rebuilt in stone, as was the gatehouse over the entrance. The archers and men-at-arms garrisoned in the Tower were kept in a state of readiness for alien attacks. In the event of a breach of the outer defences the defenders could withdraw into the keep, the only entrance to which was on the first floor. The wooden staircase which led up to the sturdy oak door could be demolished in times of danger.

The interior of the building was even more impressive, for it was designed as a royal residence. On both the entrance floor and the upper floor there were two enormous rooms—a hall and a chamber. The upper chamber contained the private apartments of the King and Queen, which were separated off with partitions and hangings. Fireplaces with outside vents had been built into the exterior walls. There were small chambers in the outer walls which contained lavatories with wooden seats on top of chutes which stuck out into space. The ground floor contained the well, and essential stores of grain, salted meat, wine, ale, tallow, hides and rope. A beautiful chapel, dedicated to St John the Evangelist, had been built into the keep itself. Faced with cream-coloured Caen stone, it reached up through two floors to the top of the Tower. Within the wall round the top storey was a gallery along which courtiers could promenade.

It was no wonder that this new and foreign palace-fortress terrified the Londoners. They were independent people with a well-developed system of local government, and they found the Tower a constant reminder of the Norman supremacy; though they might reflect that even if it had been built to subdue them, it was clearly able to defend them also.

# The Building of the Tower

The construction of a great building needed large numbers of skilled craftsmen—especially masons and carpenters—and an army of labourers to fetch and carry. Even so work would progress slowly, for medieval builders had little machinery to help them except for hoisting up materials.

The surviving buildings of the medieval Tower were built for strength rather than appearances, but within the massive White Tower is the Chapel of St John the Evangelist, a beautiful example of Norman church-building. The fine-grained stone was brought by sea from Normandy.

The stonework of St John's Chapel is plain except for the capitals of the columns, on which there are four different designs; one is shown above. 300 years later Edward III's masons built the vaulting under the Bloody Tower and carved lions' heads supporting the ribs of the vault.

# 1 Eleanor of Provence, the Young Bride

WHEN ELEANOR OF PROVENCE was betrothed at the age of fourteen to the English King, Henry III, she was deeply reluctant to leave home. Her childhood in sunny Provence had been happy. She had grown up in the company of five lively sisters in one of the most cultivated courts in Europe. Her father, Count Raymond, was a poet and patron to a host of troubadours and musicians. Eleanor, who was so beautiful that she was nicknamed "La Belle", had written an epic poem herself. It had been circulated in the courts of Europe and had received considerable acclaim.

As she journeyed to England in 1236 with her household of noblemen, ladies, servants and musicians, Eleanor prepared herself for the worst. The

English climate was said to be dismal. The court was not noted for its culture. Englishmen seemed to have few interests beyond the chase, while she herself did not know what companionship to expect from a man who had been turned down by several prospective brides.

Eleanor's first impression of the Tower of London, to which she was brought after her marriage in Canterbury Cathedral, merely confirmed her deepest prejudices. She had never seen such a chaotic castle in all her life. It consisted of a motley collection of buildings, most of which were being reconstructed. The bailey was swarming with labourers who were moving materials, mixing mortar, making lime, and fetching and carrying, while masons, carpenters and glaziers were working in huts round the edge.

Within and without the walls, the inmates of the castle were trying to get on with their daily chores. The huntsmen were feeding the falcons and exercising the hounds, men-at-arms were training with lance, sword and axe on horseback, and archers were practising at the butts. The dairymaids were milking the cows. Cooks were baking bread and turning spits in the open-air kitchens. Smiths and armourers were repairing armour, harnesses, carts and wagons in their permanent worksheds. There was a tremendous hubbub as the noise of men and animals mingled with the clang of hammer and anvil, the grating of saws, the rumble of wheels and the thudding of hooves on the cobblestones. The air was thick with conflicting smells from stored hay, roasting meat, sewage, refuse and manure.

Some buildings of distinction stood out from the chaos. The Bell Tower dominated the south-west corner, the Wakefield Tower was almost complete, and of course William the Conqueror's keep rose up sheer and startling white. Henry III had ordered it to be whitewashed all over, partly to preserve the stonework, and partly to make it look beautiful. He even ordered the lead gutters that carried water off the roof to be carried to the ground so that the white walls should not be stained.

It was not long, however, before Eleanor began to revise her opinions. From the beginning, Henry proved a loving husband and a sympathetic companion. Eleanor thought him very handsome although he had inherited the drooping eyelid of his Plantagenet forbears. He was kind and gentle by nature, and artistic by temperament. He had been interested in architecture and the arts since he was a boy, and he loved beautiful things. Henry showered his child-bride with costly dresses and jewels, and encouraged her to share his interests.

Eleanor did not need much encouragement. Once Henry unfolded his building plans to her, she understood the reasoning behind the chaos. The King was working on an outer and an inner ring of defences round the Tower. He was also trying to turn the buildings below the White Tower that housed the royal family into a proper palace. A hundred and fifty years had elapsed since the construction of the White Tower and the royal family had come to expect more spacious and comfortable accommodation than it offered. Consequently, it had moved into a collection of buildings called the "King's Houses" to the south which Henry, who spent much less time abroad than his predecessors, was determined to improve.

By the time Eleanor had arrived, Henry had already built a large kitchen and completely renovated the Great Hall where the household took their meals. Now, with the young Queen, he planned the redecoration of the royal chambers. The Queen's chamber was whitewashed and painted with flowers. When she grew tired of this, she had the room wainscoted in wood panelling and painted with roses. Henry fitted his chamber with new wooden shutters, painted with the royal arms. In more practical mood, the King and Queen organized the building of more fireplaces, garderobes or lavatories, a pentice (passageway) to the kitchen, and a sausery to store salted meat.

They also spent many happy hours planning the redecoration of the Tower's two chapels. St John's chapel in the White Tower had been unable to accommodate all the castle inhabitants and so another chapel, dedicated to St Peter ad Vincula (St Peter in chains), had been erected early in the twelfth century in the north-west corner of the bailey. Both chapels were now whitewashed inside. Stained glass was put in the windows. The wooden beams were painted in red, gold and green, and the corners were filled with gilded statues.

Henry and Eleanor also had great fun with their collection of wild animals. It all started with the gift of a Norwegian bear which was provided with a muzzle and chain and allowed to fish in the Thames. In spite of these hunting expeditions, the bear was not self-supporting and the King ordered the sheriffs of London to provide fourpence a day for its keep.

Then King Louis of France sent a gift of an elephant, which caused an even greater stir than the white bear. Finding that he did not have accommodation suitable for such an enormous beast. Henry ordered the sheriffs to build him an elephant house. Nearly a century and a half earlier, Henry I had started a park for wild animals in Woodstock, near Oxford. Henry III now had the lions, leopards and other wild animals from Woodstock transferred to the Tower and the menagerie became one of the sights of London.

The King's passion for building inevitably caused him financial difficulties. In addition to the works in the Tower, attention was being lavished on Westminster Abbey and other royal castles. Sometimes the King had to borrow money, and sometimes he was forced to economize. On more than one occasion he came into conflict with his subjects when he was building on their property. When he took in more land for the new defences, which included a moat, he had to pay compensation to the Master of St Katharine's Hospital, and to the Prior of Holy Trinity, Aldgate, amounting to £166 2s 10d.

Neither did the building itself always go smoothly. There was, for instance, the puzzling matter of the gateway in the west wall. No sooner had it been built than it fell down. It was reconstructed—and collapsed a year later on exactly the same day. There was consternation all round, especially since the incident was widely believed to have had a supernatural cause. One of the priests in the Tower claimed to have had a dream in which he had seen St Thomas à Becket strike down the gateway.

Another unfortunate occurrence was the violent death of the Tower's most important prisoner, Griffith, son of Llewellyn, the ruler of North Wales. Lodged in the former royal apartments in the White Tower, the Welsh prisoner tried to escape. Using a rope made out of sheets and strips of cloth he lowered himself out of a window at the top of the White Tower. The makeshift rope broke, and he fell to the ground with such force that his head was driven into his shoulders.

Ill omens such as these did not affect the royal couple's feelings towards the Tower, and they continued to spend a great deal of time there with their growing family of five children. Although they were not in permanent residence, the Tower had one great advantage over their other palaces— it was fortified. Henry was devout and artistic, but he was an incompetent ruler, and in due course alienated a section of the barons, as well as the citizens of London.

The more unpopular Henry became, the more he felt the need to withdraw into his stronghold in the capital. Even the security of the Tower was threatened in 1267 when the Londoners supported a baronial revolt and laid siege to it. The Queen, who was staying in the Tower at the time, tried to slip out at nightfall, but when her boat passed under London Bridge some Londoners pelted her with stones and rotten vegetables, and she was forced to return. Henry defeated the rebels, but the Queen was deeply saddened that such an incident should have occurred in the home in which she had been so happy.

# 2 John de Segrave, the Constable's Son

JOHN DE SEGRAVE was puffed up with pride when he came to the Tower of London in 1322. As newly appointed Constable, his father, Stephen de Segrave, was one of the most powerful men in the realm. The new Constable was expected to maintain himself in style and he brought his own armed retainers, attendant squires and household servants with him. The Tower inhabitants welcomed them with respect. Yet there was someone in the Tower at this time who had precedence even over the Constable. This was Edward II's beautiful Queen, Isabella of France. The King was having trouble with his unruly barons and had sent the Queen and her three eldest children, Edward, John and Eleanor, to the Tower for safety.

The Queen had recently given birth to her fourth child—a baby girl. "Joan of the Tower", as she was called, was the first person of the blood royal to be born in the Tower. Unfortunately, her birth had not taken place in fitting circumstances. The palace was in very bad repair and water had seeped through the roof of the Queen's chamber, drenching mother and baby as they lay in bed. The Constable, John Cromwell, had been dismissed for negligence, and Stephen de Segrave appointed instead.

John de Segrave was the seventh male heir in a family which had come over with William the Conqueror and had remained loyal to the monarchy ever since. Although he was only eight years old, he was well aware of the burdens his father shouldered as Constable of the Tower. To begin with, there were three high-ranking prisoners in his charge.

One was Lady Baddlesmere, who was in the Tower for insulting the Queen. A year earlier Queen Isabella, on her way back from a pilgrimage at Canterbury, had sought shelter in Leeds Castle, the Baddlesmere family seat. Lord Baddlesmere, who was in opposition to the King, happened to be away at the time, so his wife took it upon herself to refuse the Queen admittance. Not only did she deny her hospitality, but her garrisoned soldiers killed six members of the royal retinue who approached too close. Swift retribution had followed. Leeds

Castle was starved into surrender, its Constable was hanged, and Lady Baddlesmere was brought to the Tower.

The two other prisoners were powerful opponents of the King's, Roger Mortimer, eighth Baron Wigmore, and his uncle Roger Mortimer of Chirk. They were locked up together in a room in the palace, but remained a constant source of anxiety to the Constable, for they had influential friends working for them outside.

The Constable was also responsible for the security of the Mint, and the royal treasury. For the greater protection of the Mint, Edward I had moved it into the Tower during the previous reign. He had also transferred some of the royal treasures to the Tower for safer keeping after discovering that they were being stolen with the connivance of the monks of Westminster Abbey. However, he did keep some treasures and all the coronation regalia in the Abbey.

Another of the Constable's duties was to defend the liberty or jurisdiction of the Tower which did not just include the Tower and its defences, but also Tower Hill, East Smithfield and the Tower Hamlets. The inhabitants living within this area of forty-two acres had certain privileges such as freedom from arrest, and their own judicial processes. The Constable was always having to defend these privileges against the mayor and sheriffs of

London, who were very mistrustful and jealous of the independent body in their midst.

Once a year, the Constable, his officers and the inhabitants of the Tower processed round the Tower limits. Following an old Anglo-Saxon custom claiming parish jurisdiction, the Tower children whacked the boundary marks with sticks. They might even be beaten themselves to make sure that they would remember the marks in case of a future boundary dispute.

Stephen de Segrave might have found his office altogether too burdensome, had it not been for one factor. The office of Constable was a very profitable one. In addition to an annual salary, he had a variety of perquisites and privileges which brought him in a great deal of money. Every earl, baron and knight committed to his charge had to pay him a fee, and he also received money from the Exchequer for the diet of the prisoners and their attendants. If a prisoner refused the allowance it was passed on to the Constable.

He was allowed to add to his income in other curious ways. Every ship from Bordeaux carrying wine up the river Thames had to deposit two flagons on Tower Wharf. All boats bringing oysters, mussels and cockles to the city had to leave a maund (some 36 kilos) on the wharf. The Constable also had valuable fishing rights between the Tower and London Bridge. Any pig, cow, or sheep that fell off the bridge belonged to him. Any swan which came floating under the bridge towards the Tower found its way to the Constable's table. He could lay claim to all flotsam and jetsam in the same stretch of river. The tanners who dried out animal skins in East Smithfield had to pay the Constable a fee, as did anyone who wished to grow herbage on Tower Hill. All carts, whether loaded or empty, that fell into the moat became the Constable's property.

What with one thing and another, the Constable's son was never bored in the Tower, never short of entertainment. For instance, he could visit the menagerie which was housed alongside the Lion Tower at the western gate. Henry III's elephant had died, but the menagerie contained lions, leopards, bears and other animals. The sheriffs of London were still responsible for the upkeep of some of the animals. They had to pay sixpence a day for the royal lion, and sixpence for the leopard, as well as threepence a day for their keepers. John was equally fascinated by the Mint which was housed in a shed between the outer and inner walls on the western side of the Tower. Here, the coins of the realm were made under the supervision of the Master-Moneyer.

Another treasure in the Tower, as valuable in its way as the King's plate and jewels, was the collection of records which had accumulated in the White Tower. The value of these ancient rolls of parchment had not always been recognized, and they had fallen into a sorry state of muddle and decay. It was Edward II who grasped their importance as an historical collection, and he had given orders for the records to be sorted out. John would watch the clerks at work, patching, sorting, and deciphering the rolls of ancient writs, charters, lists of expenses, treaties, laws, proclamations and other memoranda.

After he had spent some two years in the Tower, John had grown used to his status. He had even begun to dream of the day when he would succeed his father as Constable, for the office had originally been an hereditary one. But John's ambitions were never to be realized. On 2 August 1324 something happened which brought his interesting and privileged life in the Tower to an abrupt end. In the early hours of the morning on that fateful day, the curfew bell above the Bell Tower rang out a warning. All was confusion in the bailey. Foot soldiers were shouting and running from place to place, while the Tower inhabitants, worried and curious, stood around in groups. The Constable could be seen gesticulating and arguing on top of the Wakefield Tower. The young Roger Mortimer had escaped.

As the morning wore on, the details of the escape became clearer. Mortimer had escaped from his room, crawled through a hole into the royal kitchen, and squeezed up the chimney place on to the roof of the palace alongside the Wakefield Tower. Working his way across the ledge of the roof he had reached the Bloody Tower and let himself down to the ground with the aid of a rope ladder. He had then negotiated the outer wall and the moat and made his getaway in a waiting boat.

Gossip and rumour followed in the wake of this dramatic escape, which had been so perfectly timed. The first day of August was the feast of St Peter ad Vincula, and the evening had been spent in festivities and drinking, so that the level of vigilance in the Tower had been at its lowest. It was obvious that Mortimer had received help from his powerful friends outside.

But what of inside? Who had drugged Mortimer's gaolers, made a hole in the wall and provided the rope ladder? Suspicion fell on several people, including Gerard Alspath, a Warwickshire neighbour of de Segrave's who had accompanied him to the Tower. It was even rumoured that Queen Isabella herself had connived in the escape.

In spite of the rumours, it was the Constable who was severely reprimanded. Edward II immediately removed de Segrave from his office in the Tower. He was bound over to pay a fine of £10,000 and was summoned to serve abroad in the war in France. Young John de Segrave, who had come to the Tower so full of pride, felt the disgrace keenly, for his family never recovered its greatness.

A year later the Queen went to France where she

# The Defences of the Tower

Very rarely were castles taken
at the first attack; either
the defenders decided they were
bound to be overwhelmed
eventually and surrendered, or
there was a drawn-out siege
when the attackers used
throwing engines to break down
the walls before trying to put
up scaling ladders.

Tower defences included portcullises (this one below the Bloody Tower still works), watergates (the one under St Thomas's Tower became famous as Traitors' Gate) and drawbridges (this one beside the Byward Tower survived until the moat was drained in 1843).

became intimate with the escaped prisoner Roger Mortimer. She persuaded her oldest son Edward to join her there. In 1326 they returned to England and raised an army against Edward II. The King was captured, deposed and later brutally murdered in Berkeley Castle. Edward III succeeded his father as king, but for nearly four years he was merely a puppet ruler in the hands of Isabella and Mortimer. In October 1330 the young king managed to assert himself, and Mortimer was captured while staying in Nottingham Castle. Mortimer was brought to the Tower as a prisoner for the second time and after being tried and convicted for treason he was hanged at Tyburn.

# 3 The Black Prince

THE TOWER OF LONDON played an important role in the Hundred Years War, both as the chief arsenal of the realm, and as a prison. Edward of Woodstock, known since Elizabethan times as the Black Prince, got to know the Tower well during the early stages of this long intermittent struggle against the French, for although the Tower was not his permanent residence, he often stayed there. From the age of eight, Edward was appointed Keeper of the Realm whenever his father, Edward III, was abroad. He did not actually make decisions, but the Council could not meet without his presence.

The Black Prince was well suited for the martial age in which he grew up. His imagination was fired by war, and his ambition was to become a great soldier like his father. He was strong and well-developed for his age, and under the direction of his Master-in-Arms he worked hard at all the martial skills so that he would be well prepared for the day when he would go to the wars. He rode in armour, engaged in sword-play, and perfected his jousting techniques against a swivelling target called a quintain. He spent days out hunting and hawking on his horse, Bayard Rous, which helped sharpen his senses.

At the same time he studied the code of chivalry, for it took more than skill at arms to be a knight. The chivalric code of behaviour dictated that a perfect knight should be loyal, honourable and courteous, as well as skilful and courageous in battle. Edward tried to develop these qualities in his everyday life. Under the influence of his mother, Queen Philippa of Hainault, he took his religion very seriously. Because he had been born near Trinity Sunday, he was placed under the care of the Trinity rather than a patron saint. As Trinity Sunday was associated with the Martyrdom of St Thomas à Becket, Edward often went on pilgrimage to Becket's shrine at Canterbury.

Edward was the eldest of a growing number of sisters and brothers. Next to him in age came Isabella, then Joan. William died young, but Lionel and John were strong and healthy. Queen Philippa, though an affectionate mother, sometimes left her children in order to go on campaign with her husband: in 1342, for instance, she accompanied him to France.

The Black Prince was still too young to go, but he was old enough to take an interest in the Tower's war effort. The Tower served as a storehouse for the arms and armour needed in the field. The King made demands on the store when he needed weapons. John de Flete, who was Keeper of the Privy Wardrobe, was responsible for the arms that were brought to the Tower by country sheriffs, purchased, or transferred from other areas. His hardest task was to maintain the supply of bowstaves and arrows needed by the English archers.

Certain manufacturing activities were also being carried out in the Tower. The artillers, for instance, produced crossbows, a larger version of the crossbow called a balista, and traditional artillery engines like the catapult and trebuchet. They were also working with a dangerous explosive called gunpowder on new "secret" weapons which shot iron balls or bolts. Other craftsmen were making the padded tunics worn by the archers, the leather boxes and quivers for the arrows, the ropes and canvas and all the extras needed for war.

After Mass on Sundays every able-bodied man and boy in the Tower had to gather at the butts for archery practice. This had been made compulsory by Edward I, who had seen the potential of the Welsh longbow, but had realized that it was a weapon requiring unusual skill. The garrisoned soldiers in steel hats and padded tunics moved among the novices giving advice and demonstrating techniques. The best among them could loose an arrow twelve times a minute and hit the target every time.

When the Prince was fifteen years old, the summons he had been so eagerly awaiting came at last, and he went first to Flanders and then to France with his father. In August of the following year, the English won a great victory over the French at Crecy. Throughout his first battle the Prince fought with exceptional valour. At one point he was in great personal danger and his protector sent a messenger to the King to ask for help. The King, who had recently knighted his son, wished him to prove himself, so instead of throwing in a reserve he returned the message, "Let him take pains to win his spurs and to be worthy of the honour of knighthood which I so lately conferred upon him."

The return of the King and Prince in October 1347 was marked by a round of entertainments and celebrations. Nineteen tournaments were held in a period of seven months. These chivalrous combats were very popular now that Edward had created his own round table of knights (which included the Black Prince) and invested them with the Order of the Garter. The lavish festivities were partly intended to impress the foreigners now being kept in honourable captivity in the Tower of London.

Among them were the Count d'Eu, the Constable of France, the Count de Tankerville, and King David II of Scotland, who was married to "Joan of the Tower", the King's younger sister. He had taken advantage of the King's involvement in France to invade England, but had been defeated at Neville's Cross. Prisoners such as these were received at the Tower by the Constable, Sir John Darcy, and were housed with their servants and attendants in all possible comfort in the various towers. They could secure their freedom as soon as their huge ransoms had been paid off.

The frivolities were brought to an abrupt end in the late autumn of 1348 by the plague. This dread disease killed not in ones and twos but in hundreds and thousands. It had been raging in the south of England since the summer. It was called the Black Death because those who caught it developed swellings under their arms and in their groins, and then came out in blackish spots from which they seldom recovered. The city bells started ringing for the dead on November the first, All Saints Day. So many deaths followed that the church bells fell silent, and burial ceremonies ceased. Corpses were piled on to carts and flung into communal ditches.

When the first victim died in the Tower, an eerie atmosphere fell on the place. Many people died within the walls, including numerous craftsmen, Robert le Bowyere, who was Keeper of the King's

Lions, and two brother masons, John and William Ramsey. Most work came to a standstill through lack of will, manpower, and materials, and the Tower began to look neglected. Stores and provisions were used up and not replenished, stonework crumbled and was not restored, manure and refuse festered and stank in heaps within the grounds. Not even the Tower's traditional scavengers, the black ravens, could dispose of it.

The royal family itself was not spared. In July 1348 Edward's second sister Joan had been sent off to Spain to marry Pedro, the heir to the throne of Castile. The journey was so long that the fourteen-year-old girl and her retinue had broken the journey at Bordeaux. There she caught the plague and died. The whole family was deeply saddened by her death, for she had been a sweet-natured child.

When the plague had died down and hostilities with France were resumed, the Tower had to work overtime to replenish the depleted stock of weapons. It took William de Rothwell seven years of hard work to revitalize the arsenal. His efforts were rewarded, for in 1356 the English, under the command of the Black Prince, won a resounding victory at Poitiers. Among the French prisoners captured in the battle was King John II of France himself. Ordinary soldiers who were not worth a ransom were slaughtered without mercy, but knights were as usual treated with care.

The chivalrous way in which the Black Prince treated the French King made him famous throughout Christendom. After the battle he gave a dinner at which the French King was seated in the place of honour, while he himself sat at a lower table. With even greater humility, he insisted upon serving the King with his own hands. When he returned to England in the following year, he continued to behave modestly towards his captive.

The Londoners gave him a fantastic welcome. The mayor, aldermen and members of the guilds wore new clothes for the occasion. The streets were hung with tapestries and banners. Twelve girls were suspended in gilded cages above the route to scatter flowers on the hero. The fountains ran with red and white wine. The King of France was mounted on a superb white charger, while the Prince rode behind him on a small black hackney. At Westminster, the King of England waited to congratulate his son.

Poitiers was the last great victory in Edward III's reign. The King gradually fell into senility and by the time he died in 1377 nearly all the possessions won by the English had been lost. The Black Prince contracted a fever from which he never recovered. He was forced to retire from the wars, and died prematurely a year before his father, leaving his ten-year-old son Richard to succeed to the throne.

# The Armoury

A knight in the time of the Black Prince wore, next to his body, a quilted tunic, then a sleeved mail shirt, then a "coat of plates" to protect his chest and back. On top he wore a "coat of arms" with his heraldic device.

Mail was made by riveting together the ends of interlocking metal rings. Helmets were made in one piece, but the great helm, worn over the helmet or instead of it, was made up of five plates.

The English longbow was made of yew; arrows were of ash, flighted with grey goose feathers. There were differently shaped arrow heads for different targets—for cutting or smashing or piercing.

The earliest picture of a gun, dating from 1326, shows a vase-cannon. The guns in the lower picture, almost 150 years later, look more familiar. But both handguns and cannons were still fired simply by putting a match to the touch hole.

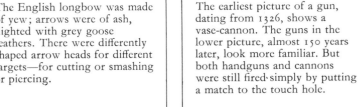

## 4 Richard II and the Peasants Revolt

KING RICHARD II was fourteen years old when the Peasants Revolt broke out in 1381. As soon as the King's council heard of the rising, they removed themselves and the young King to the Tower of London. There they felt secure. The Tower was considered to be impregnable and had never yet been taken by force. They intended to sit tight until the uprising had blown over.

But instead of blowing over, the revolt started to spread. The rebels had acquired two magnetic leaders in Wat Tyler, and a radical preacher called John Ball. On 10 June they occupied Canterbury, plundered the Cathedral, and wrecked the apartments of Archbishop Simon Sudbury, who as Chancellor of England was one of their chief targets.

They frightened Rochester Castle into surrender, and by taking his children as hostage forced the Constable, Sir John Newton, to accompany them to London.

Meanwhile more noblemen were taking refuge in the Tower. With the King were most of his advisers, including Sudbury, the Treasurer Robert Hales, and the Lords Warwick, Salisbury, Arundel and Suffolk. The most notable absence was that of John of Gaunt, who was away in Scotland. For companions Richard had his two half-brothers, the young Earl of Oxford, and his cousin Henry Bolingbroke. The King's mother Joan of Kent reached the safety of the Tower just in time. She had been visiting holy shrines in Kent, and on the way home had encountered the rebels, who had had the impertinence to kiss her and some of her ladies.

Though the rebels were on their way to London, the rulers of the realm continued to feel safe in the Tower. As a result of Edward III's improvements it was in a good state of repair. The Constable was loyal, and the military establishment, swelled by the armed retainers of the nobility, numbered some six hundred men—well above its usual strength. No one envisaged a siege, for it was taken for granted that William Walworth, the loyal mayor of London, would be able to keep the city defences up against the rebels.

They were mistaken. Not only did the rebels

reach the outskirts of London, but by a combination of pressure from without and treachery from within they crossed London Bridge and entered the city. From a turret in the White Tower the King and his courtiers watched their destructive progress as they rampaged through the streets towards the Tower. When night drew in the rebels settled themselves down on Tower Hill and in St Katharine's Hospital on the other side, in defiant proximity to the Tower.

While the crowd moved restlessly around outside, the King and his council sat down to discuss their predicament; but so stunned and frightened were they that they could not make up their minds what to do. One faction wanted to fight a way out of London, while the other wanted to stay. As the arguments flew back and forth the King was seized with a feeling of destiny. All at once he knew what had to be done, and that he could do it. He would go out in person and face the rebels. They would not harm him. After all, was he not their anointed monarch, and they his loyal subjects?

From the day he had succeeded to the throne at the age of ten, Richard had been King in name only. He had been dominated by his uncle John of Gaunt, and had grown up in the shadow of his famous father, the Black Prince. His mother, Joan of Kent, wished her sensitive, artistic son to be brought up in the martial traditions of his father. By her previous marriage to Sir Thomas Holland she had two sons, the Earl of Kent and Sir John Holland, who were held up to Richard as paragons of chivalry. Now at last a chance had arisen for Richard to assert himself, and the older men around the table agreed to the risky plan.

Richard's resolve did not weaken in the restless hours that followed, and at seven o'clock the following morning he left the Tower for Mile End where most of the rebels, with the exception of a contingent that stayed behind, were waiting for him. The King's nerve held from the beginning, even when Thomas Farringdon, the leader of the Essex men, clung to his bridle. He moved on at a steady pace without panic. His half-brothers were made of less stern stuff. Holland and Kent edged away from the royal party and galloped away as soon as they got the opportunity.

In the open space of Mile End an enormous crowd was gathered. Undaunted, the slender boy rode straight towards them to conduct a conversation.

"My friends, I am your King and your Lord. What do you want? And what do you wish to say?"

Their reply was, "We want you to set us free for ever, us and our descendants and our lands, and to grant that we should never again be serfs nor held in bondage."

The King agreed to all their demands and promised them a general pardon if they would return quietly to their homes. When they began to disperse, the royal party, full of relief at the safe outcome of the meeting, started back for the Tower.

On the way, they received the most appalling news. While the King had been talking to the rebels at Mile End, the others who had been left behind walked into the Tower. The drawbridges were down and they entered the west gate without encountering the least resistance from the soldiers whose duty it was to guard the fortress.

They had broken into the royal apartments, upturned the royal bed, ransacked the wardrobe and insulted the King's mother. She had been put in a boat and was now safely installed in the Queen's Wardrobe, a building near St Paul's.

Other servants of the King were not so lucky. The Chancellor, Simon Sudbury, and the Treasurer, Robert Hales, were dragged out of St John's Chapel where they were praying, taken to Tower Hill and beheaded. Sudbury's execution was particularly brutal, for it took eight strokes of the axe to severe his head. The heads of the victims were put on stakes and carried by the rebels in triumph through the streets of London before being impaled on London Bridge.

When he heard of the disaster which had befallen his fortress, the King decided not to return there but to join his mother instead.

They could not understand the events in the

Tower. There were too many questions that needed explanations. Why had the drawbridge not been raised after the King's departure for Mile End? Why had the soldiers stood by when the rebels rushed in? Had they been bribed or persuaded, or simply taken by surprise? The facts remained that the Tower had been invaded, the palace had been soiled; the sanctuary of the chapel royal had been violated, and blood had been spilt on Tower Hill.

All through the night the mob continued to terrorize the city. The situation seemed desperate and the King's advisers did not know what to do. Once again Richard took the initiative by suggesting that he confront the rebels. At this point, the councillors should have called upon the loyal citizens, who had had enough of the mob, to take up arms against them, but they feebly agreed to the King's plan, although it would put him in the most fearful jeopardy.

The King himself was not blind to the danger. The next morning he rode to Westminster Abbey to hear Mass and to make his confession. Then, with some two hundred followers who had taken the precaution of wearing armour under their clothes, he rode out to Smithfield where the rebels were convened.

The manner in which Wat Tyler presented the rebels' complaints was clumsy, but all might have gone well had not one of the King's supporters objected to the coarse way in which he mounted his pony and drank ale in front of the King. A scuffle broke out and Tyler was mortally wounded. He spurred his horse forward, crying to the common people to avenge him, then fell half dead to the ground.

"They have cut down our captain," cried his followers. "Come on, let us kill them all."

The situation was explosive. The King and his followers were in an enclosed space, vastly out-numbered by an army of angry peasants who were bending their bows and drawing swords and daggers. But it was not an experienced soldier or loyal councillor who took command and prevented a massacre. It was a boy of fourteen. Richard II rode towards the rebels all by himself crying,

"You have no other captain but me. I am your King. Keep the peace."

His words had a magical effect on the peasants. Some began to disperse and Richard led the rest out to Clerkenwell Fields. When the King returned to the Wardrobe his mother met him,

"Ah, fair son, what pain and anguish have I had for you this day!" she cried.

"Certes, madam, I know it well," replied the King. "But now rejoice and praise God, for today I have recovered my heritage and the realm of England, the which I had near lost."

He was not exaggerating, and he had every right

to be proud of himself. Throughout the crisis he had acted with amazing courage. He had shown himself more than worthy of his illustrious father.

The dramatic events of 1381 proved a high point in Richard's reign. His subsequent neurotic and tyrannical behaviour resulted in constant opposition from the barons until finally in 1399 he was forced to abdicate the throne in favour of his cousin Henry Bolingbroke. It was ironic that the abdication ceremony took place in the same council chamber in the White Tower where, years earlier, Richard in the presence of his cousin had conducted himself so forcefully.

# Tudor London and the Tower

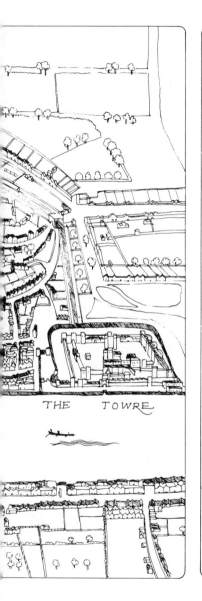

THE TOWRE

The earliest surviving detailed, and more or less reliable, map of London was published in 1572. Most Londoners still lived in the square mile within the Roman walls which had been repaired during the Middle Ages, but suburbs were beginning to grow—like Southwark at the other end of London Bridge and Stepney east of the Tower. Details on the map include Old St Paul's with its great steeple and, south of the river, the rings for bull and bear baiting. As in medieval times the Tower was still London's outstanding landmark.

# 5 The Little Princes

WHEN EDWARD V CAME to the Tower in 1483 to prepare for his coronation, he was a boy of twelve. He entered London riding by the side of his uncle Richard, Duke of Gloucester, was acclaimed as King by the people, taken to the Tower and installed in the palace with a large retinue to serve him.

Under the direction of Peter Curteys, Keeper of the Wardrobe, the preparations for the coronation went ahead. Edward was measured and fitted in velvets, satins, and cloth of gold. Step by step he was taken through the traditional coronation ceremonial so that when the great day came he would be well rehearsed.

On the surface, everything appeared to be in order, but Edward was dogged by a feeling of unease. He could not forget what had happened on the journey from London to Wales after he had heard of the unexpected death of his father, Edward IV. At Stony Stratford the royal party had been intercepted by the Duke of Gloucester and the Duke of Buckingham. Richard of Gloucester had been Edward IV's favourite brother and trusted right-hand man. The new king had no reason to mistrust him, for Richard had treated his nephew affectionately, but at the same time he had arrested the men who had been in charge of him. Edward had protested tearfully, but his uncle had not heeded him.

Now in the Tower, Edward felt very lonely. His mother, the Queen, had taken refuge in the Sanctuary of Westminster Abbey with his unmarried sisters and his younger brother Richard, Duke of York, and refused to come out, and Edward was isolated from all his immediate family except for Gloucester.

The fact of the matter was that the Queen was very unpopular. When Edward IV had married Elizabeth Woodville she had been endowed with great beauty but no royal blood. She had used her position as Queen in the most ruthless way to advance her numerous family of seven sisters, five brothers, and two sons by her first marriage.

As soon as the protection of Edward IV had been removed, the ancient nobility thirsted for the blood of the upstart Woodville clan. Foremost in their hatred of the Woodvilles were Richard of Gloucester and the Duke of Buckingham. The latter had been married off to one of the Queen's sisters when he was very young, and deeply resented it.

The tensions between Gloucester and the supporters of the Woodvilles came to a head suddenly on 13 June. On that day the Lord Protector summoned a meeting of the council in the White Tower. In the course of the meeting, Richard of Gloucester suddenly accused some of those present of plotting with the Woodvilles against himself, and at a prearranged signal a band of armed guards rushed into the chamber crying "Treason! Treason!"

In the struggle that followed, Bishop Morton, Archbishop Rotherham, Lord Stanley and Lord Hastings, who was Lord Chamberlain, were overpowered. The Bishop of Ely and the Archbishop of York were escorted to prison quarters in the Tower. Stanley was put under house arrest. Hastings was told to prepare for instant death. A priest was found so that he could make a brief confession, after which he was led out to the green by the chapel of St Peter ad Vincula, where his head was chopped off on a piece of wood that had been left lying about by some carpenters.

Poor Edward did not know what to make of these events. He had been shocked at the way in which his uncle had turned against the Woodvilles, but at the same time the Protector took great pains to protest his affection and loyalty. A few days later he even took the trouble to provide Edward with a companion and playmate—Richard, Duke of York. At first Edward, who was starved of young company, was overjoyed to see his younger brother, but when he heard how Richard had been brought to the Tower he began to have the gravest misgivings. The Queen had handed the boy over with obvious reluctance, at the request of the Archbishop of Canterbury who had been sent to Westminster Abbey to persuade her, with the help of an armed guard.

Edward knew now that he could no longer trust his uncle. He suspected that the Protector had more sinister motives in bringing Richard to the Tower than simply to give him a companion.

He was not kept in suspense for long. On 22 June a sermon was delivered at St Paul's Cross declaring that Edward IV's marriage to Elizabeth Woodville was not valid, which meant that their children were bastards and Edward was not entitled to be king. Parliament petitioned Richard to accept the crown, and he moved into the Tower to prepare for his own coronation on 6 July. In all these moves he had been openly supported by the Duke of Buckingham.

Edward's own status changed overnight. One day he was King, the next he was not. One day he was called "Your Grace", the next merely "Lord Edward" or even "Bastard" Edward. Though still within the Tower, the princes had moved from a world of freedom, light and pleasure to one of confinement, darkness and misery. From their new world they were well aware of what was happening in the old. They knew that the usurper was feasting and celebrating. They knew that he was performing all the pre-coronation rites for which Edward had been preparing. On the eve before the procession, Richard III created seventeen Knights of the Bath in accordance with an ancient tradition.

On 5 July, from a concealed position, the princes watched the coronation procession leave the Tower for Westminster. Richard was splendidly attired in a long gown of purple velvet lined with ermine over a doublet of blue cloth of gold "wrought with nets and pineapples". His Queen was dressed in yards and yards of Venetian lace, while the Duke of Buckingham outshone them all in blue velvet emblazoned with golden cartwheels.

Meanwhile the princes were kept out of sight. They were not allowed to stroll about or practice archery on the green. They had no tutors to guide them, no friends to divert them and no family to comfort them. The only contact they had with the outside world was through the few ignorant servants who looked after them, and a Dr Argentine who paid them an occasional visit. Richard, especially, missed family life. Unlike Edward, he had not been brought up in a separate establishment, but had remained with his mother, although he had been married at the age of six to little Anne Mowbray, the daughter of the Duke of Norfolk.

Edward did his best to comfort Richard, but he found it hard to keep his spirits up, for he was certain that they were now in mortal danger. As rightful heirs to the throne, he and Richard were a threat to whoever sat upon it. How could they be permitted to live? He could not help brooding on the fate of his forbears who had met with violent deaths. Edward II had been deposed, then murdered. Three months after his abdication, Richard II had died of starvation. More recently there had been two deaths in the Tower itself. The Lancastrian King Henry VI had been stabbed to death while at prayer in the oratory of the Wakefield Tower, and Edward's own uncle, the Duke of Clarence, had been secretly dispatched in the Bowyer Tower.

Edward knew his uncle Richard to be a ruthless man who had rid himself of Woodville opposition and then usurped the crown. Would he stop short of shedding infant blood? There were others whom Edward feared too. There was the ambitious Duke of Buckingham, who, as a descendant of Thomas Woodstock, the youngest son of Edward III, had an indirect claim to the throne. And lying low in France was a young adventurer Edward had not met. His name was Henry Tudor, and as the nearest relation to Henry VI he was waiting to regain the crown for the Lancastrians.

Edward faced the possibility of death with incredible courage. Dr Argentine, who was his last attendant, said that "the young King like a victim prepared for sacrifice, and sought remission of his sins by daily confession and penance." Though Edward expected death, he had no idea how it would come. Would he and Richard be poisoned? Would their heads be chopped off with an axe? Would they be hanged by their necks with a rope, or smothered while they slept?

The fate of the princes remains a mystery. No one will ever know for certain exactly how, or in what tower, they were murdered. What is known is that they were not seen in the Tower after the month of July 1483. By August, rumours that they had been murdered had started to circulate in London.

In 1485 Richard III was killed in the Battle of Bosworth and Henry Tudor became Henry VII. It was during his reign that the detailed story of how the princes were murdered on the instructions of Richard III, was publicly circulated. Two centuries later, in the reign of Charles II, some human bones, mixed up with animal bones, were found in a chest under a staircase leading up to St John's Chapel in the White Tower. The remains were examined by the royal surgeon and some skilled antiquaries, who came to the conclusion that they were the skeletons of Edward and Richard. Charles II had them re-interred in Westminster Abbey.

In 1933 the bones were exhumed, and a further examination took place. The bones were then attributed to children of about thirteen and ten, but they cannot be precisely identified. Meanwhile, the Tudor version of the story has not stood up to modern historical scrutiny. Which of the three suspects— Richard III, Henry VII, or the Duke of Buckingham—was the guilty party is still a matter for debate and speculation.

# Tournaments

Henry set up a royal armoury workshop near his palace at Greenwich, which went on making armours for Kings and courtiers for 120 years. Some of the finest of them are now in the White Tower.

Henry VIII was proud of his strength and skill in the tournament. He had an armour made for him (called a garniture) which could be adapted for different uses in the tournament and in battle, by adding on or taking away different pieces. Here the garniture is converted for the tilt, fought with lances on horseback, and for the foot combat with poleaxes.

# 6 Margaret Roper and Sir Thomas More

MARGARET ROPER'S FIRST VISIT to the Tower was in May 1534, when she came to see her father, Sir Thomas More, who was imprisoned there. Her heart was bursting with fearful anticipation and emotion. She had not seen her adored father for over a month, and she did not know how she would find him, for the only communication that she had received from him was a note of love written with a charred stick on a scrap of paper. More was in prison because as a loyal Catholic he had refused to recognize King Henry VIII's right to divorce his first wife Catherine of Aragon and then his actions making himself head of the church in England.

In fact, Margaret found her father wonderfully unchanged. He was thinner but not repining.

Indeed, he almost seemed to be enjoying his imprisonment, for it gave him a chance to concentrate on the spiritual life he had neglected when he held public office. Now at last he had time to write and to pray and do penance with hair shirt and scourge.

He had entered the grim fortress as cheerfully as if he was visiting a friend's house. Among those waiting to receive him on the steps of Traitors' Gate were the Lieutenant, Sir Edward Walsingham, the Gentleman Porter and the Gentleman Gaoler. More had greeted the Lieutenant warmly, for they were old friends. Then he had cracked a joke with the Porter, who in accordance with ancient custom asked for More's upper garment as a perquisite. More had gravely handed over his cap so that the unfortunate man was forced to explain that he was referring to his gown—an item of greater value.

At first Margaret was shocked by his stark cold cell in the Bell Tower, which lay behind the richly furnished rooms of the Lieutenant's Lodging, but she soon forgot her dismay in the warmth of her father's presence. As soon as they were alone they knelt and recited prayers together. Only then did More allow himself the pleasure of hearing the family news, of which there was a great deal, for the household at Chelsea was a large one. He asked eagerly after his dear wife Alice, and wanted news of all his children. Margaret herself, who was married to John Roper, Elizabeth, Cecily and John all lived at Chelsea with their spouses and children. Only two members of the family had moved away from home, his stepdaughter Alice, and his adopted daughter Margaret who had married John Clement.

More told his daughter of his concern for Bishop Fisher who was imprisoned on the floor above him. Like More, John Fisher had been locked up for refusing to take the oath of succession. There was no direct communication between the two floors, and the two men had been forbidden to correspond with one another. But More knew from his servant that Fisher, who was seventy years old, had fewer comforts even than he did and was feeling the cold dreadfully.

Deep in conversation, they were hardly aware that John á Wood, More's servant, had crept in to light the candles. When the ancient bell at the top of the tower rang for curfew, they were astonished to find how quickly their time together had flown. Margaret thanked Wood for his care of her father. Out of the ten shillings a week More was paying for himself, and the five shillings he was paying for his servant, few luxuries could be purchased; but Wood was doing what he could to get kindling, candles and one adequate meal a day. Although he could not read or write, it was Wood who had smuggled his master's first letter out of the Tower.

It was terrible parting from her father, for Margaret was sure that she would not be allowed to see him again. To her surprise she was given permission to write and to visit on a number of occasions. Thomas Cromwell, the King's chief minister, had ulterior motives for encouraging these communications. He knew that Margaret was very close to her father, and he thought she might persuade him to take the oath, as she herself was prepared to take it (though with a saving clause). In one letter she did try and make him forsake his conscience, but it caused him such distress that she never raised the matter again.

Lady Alice was not so tactful. Practical by nature, she had no time for her husband's high principles and gave him a good scolding when she visited him. She was amazed that More, who was regarded as a wise man, should be such a fool as to give up his garden, library and family at Chelsea for a filthy prison infested with rats and mice. She could not see why he did not take the oath as the other bishops and learned men of the realm had done. More's reply, "Is not this house as nigh Heaven as mine own?" reduced her to muttering "Tilly vally, tilly vally" in exasperation.

Margaret was allowed further visits during the summer months, for More's imprisonment had been relaxed. He was no longer kept a close prisoner and was invited to take meals at the Lieutenant's table, stroll about in the Tower precincts and worship in St Peter ad Vincula. His ink and paper were restored to him and he was able to continue working on his religious treatises. In November 1534 two new acts were passed which required an oath acknowledging that the King was Supreme Head of the Church of England, and made it treason to deny this. Although More was too clever to deny the Supremacy outright, it was plain that he had not undergone a change of heart and he was confined to his cell again.

When Margaret was unexpectedly given a visiting pass on 5 May in the following year, she was shocked by her father's appearance. He looked shrunken and ill and his hair had turned white. While father and daughter were together on this occasion they saw a horrible sight out of the cell window overlooking Water Lane. Some Carthusian monks who had denied the Supremacy were being tied down on to the hurdles which were to draw them to Tyburn for hanging and quartering. The sight in no way weakened More's resolve. A fortnight later he was brought to trial in Westminster Hall. Although he defended himself brilliantly, false evidence was brought against him, and he was condemned to death.

He was brought back to the Tower by boat, but as the tide had turned he was landed on Tower Wharf instead of Traitors' Gate. Margaret was waiting in the crowd in the hope of seeing him. The procession was headed by the Yeoman Gaoler who was carrying the ceremonial axe with the axe edge turned inwards to indicate that the prisoner was under sentence of death. Behind him walked More and Sir William Kingston, the Constable of the Tower. They were hedged about with guards carrying halberds.

By the Old Swan Inn, the kindly Constable took his leave of More with tears running down his cheeks. Margaret could contain herself no longer. She pushed through the crowd, dodged past the guards, flung herself into her father's arms and kissed him. More blessed and comforted her, but when the guards started showing signs of impatience he parted from her and walked on. Margaret could not bear to let him go. She rushed forward and embraced him for the last time.

More's family had been informed of the date of execution and had been given permission to bury the body in the chapel of St Peter ad Vincula. For this royal favour they were deeply grateful, for they knew what indignities could happen to the bodies of people executed on Tower Hill, or at Tyburn. Only a fortnight earlier poor Fisher's body had been left lying on the scaffold all day until some soldiers buried it in a makeshift grave outside All Hallows' Church by the Tower.

Margaret pleaded to be allowed one final visit. When this was refused, she sent her maid Dorothy Colly to the Tower every day in the hope that she might be able to wheedle her way inside. The tactic worked and a friendly warder allowed her in for a short time the day before the execution. It was to her that More entrusted the mementos he was leaving to his family, his hair shirt and scourge, and his last letter to Margaret in which he wrote,

"I never liked your manner toward me better than when you kissed me last."

Margaret could not bear to see her father die. The only member of the family who witnessed the scene was Margaret Clement, More's adopted daughter. She saw More leave the Tower by the Bulwark Gate. He was wearing a coarse grey gown and looked haggard and old, but upon his face was an expression of peace and hope. His sense of humour stayed with him to the last. On seeing how rickety the temporary wooden scaffold was, he turned to the Lieutenant and said,

"I pray you, sir, see me safe up, and for my coming down let me shift for myself."

After More had made a brief speech, the executioner, dressed all in black, asked for his forgiveness for what he was going to do. More forgave him, paid him with a gold angel and made a joke about the shortness of his neck. When his eyes were bandaged he knelt down and placed his head on the block. He carefully arranged his straggling grey beard over the edge, saying, "Pity that were cut, for it hath committed no treason." The axe came down, and the executioner picked up the head from the sawdust and held it up for all to see.

The crowd, having enjoyed a morning's entertainment, began to disperse, but Margaret Clement stayed where she was, her eyes fixed to the scaffold. She saw the executioner remove the gown from More's body, for he was allowed to keep it as a perquisite of his job. When the headless body had been lowered into a wooden chest she accompanied it to the chapel of St Peter ad Vincula where Margaret Roper was waiting. They were later joined by Dorothy Colly who had been out to purchase a winding sheet. The three women prepared the body for burial, keeping back the bloodstained undershirt as a relic. They remained kneeling in the chapel long after the coffin had been placed beneath the flagstones.

For the next month Margaret Roper kept a close watch on her father's head which had been stuck on a spike on London Bridge. Every day she would approach by boat and check that it was still there, for she was determined to get hold of it before it was thrown in the river. When at last she learnt it was due to be removed to make room for others, she managed to bribe a custodian of the bridge to give it to her, and she preserved it as a relic.

Margaret survived her father by only nine years. After his death she had longed only for the day when she would meet him in Heaven where, as he had so often promised her, they would be "merry for ever and have not trouble after."

# Guns at the Tower

Henry VIII built up a great store of handguns and cannons at the Tower. Soon he invaded France, where his army besieged and captured Boulogne.

The guns used by Henry's infantry were matchlocks. When the trigger was pressed the burning end of the "match" was lowered on to the priming powder. The explosion fired the main charge in the barrel.

There was a cannon foundry at the Tower in Henry VIII's time. Guns were cast by pouring molten brass or iron into a wooden mould buried in sand. All the King's guns carried his badge, the Tudor rose.

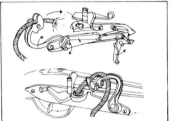

# 7 Princess Elizabeth

WHEN PRINCESS ELIZABETH LEARNT that she was to be sent to the Tower of London as a prisoner she was horrified. The Tower almost certainly meant death. In desperation she looked for delaying tactics. She requested an interview with her sister Queen Mary, but was refused. Then she begged to be allowed to write a letter, and took so long over it that the tide turned and the journey from Westminster to the Tower could not be made that day. However, no excuses were permitted on the next day, Palm Sunday 1554, and her boat set off for the dreaded fortress.

It was the most dismal journey, for the sky was grey and it was pouring with rain. As the boat drew nearer to the Tower the fate of her mother and her cousin were in the forefront of Elizabeth's mind. Anne Boleyn had been executed on Tower Green before Elizabeth had reached the age of three. King Henry VIII had granted his Queen only one request—to die by the sword instead of the axe. Poor Lady Jane Grey had been executed in the more conventional way only a week ago. Elizabeth had known her cousin well, for at one time they had had lessons together. Now that she felt so close to death herself, she could well imagine the agony of the gentle girl as she groped round blindly for the scaffold crying "Where is it? Where is it?"

When the boat landed at Traitors' Gate Elizabeth refused to get out, protesting that she was no traitor and that the water would be over her shoes. The Marquess of Winchester, in whose charge she was, told her that she had no choice in the matter. The Princess disdainfully refused the cloak he offered her and stepped uncovered into the rain, declaring,

"Here landeth as true a subject, being a prisoner, as ever landed at these stairs; and before Thee, O God, I speak it, having none other friends but Thee alone!"

The Constable, the Lieutenant, armed soldiers and warders were lined up on the landing stage to receive her. The Warders looked very impressive in the same red uniforms as the Yeoman of the Guard of which they had become a part in the reign of Edward VI. To these forbidding men Elizabeth addressed herself, once more declaring her innocence. Her apparent sincerity, her youth and her fresh appearance struck to the heart of at least one of these hardened onlookers. He called out, "God preserve Your Grace."

A few steps further on Elizabeth sank to the ground.

"Madam," advised Sir John Brydges, the Lieutenant, "you were best to come out of the rain, for you sit unwholesomely."

"It is better sitting here than in a worse place," answered the Princess, "for God knoweth, I know not, whither you will bring me."

In fact, they brought her to the Lieutenant's Lodgings where Anne Boleyn had slept before her execution. They led her along the corridor on the second floor right past the room where her mother had spent her last hours listening to the sound of the scaffold being erected outside. They locked her inside the cell on the upper floor of the Bell Tower where poor Bishop Fisher had suffered in her father's reign.

Elizabeth was something of an actress and had played the part of injured innocence to the full, but she was genuinely frightened and had cause to be. Queen Mary was jealous of Elizabeth's youth, wit and beauty, and resentful of her birth. She could not forgive her for being the daughter of Anne Boleyn, who had ousted her own mother Catherine of Aragon from the throne.

But a more important difference between the two sisters was religion. Mary was a devout Catholic, intent on bringing England back into the Catholic fold. Elizabeth made a pretence of attending Mass, but she was a Protestant at heart. Although she was careful to have nothing to do with malcontents, she became a symbol for Protestant opposition to Mary. This had come to a head after the announcement of the Queen's intended marriage with the Catholic King Philip II of Spain, for rebellions broke out in various parts of the country, and Elizabeth was put in the Tower under suspicion of being involved in them. She knew that Mary would be reluctant to have her executed unless she could gather evidence of her involvement and prove a case against her. This evidence Elizabeth was determined not to provide, no matter what her circumstances.

And these proved extremely unnerving. Her cell was cramped, bare and cold, though Elizabeth's two servants did what they could to make it more habitable. They kindled a fire in the fireplace at one end, spread straw on the bare floor and hung tapestries over the open windows to keep the wind out. Her servants were allowed to prepare her food outside, but were compelled to hand it over to the guards at the main gate. It was not surprising that not much was left by the time it reached Elizabeth. Complaints were made, and Elizabeth's servants were finally allowed to bring in the food themselves and prepare it in the Lieutenant's kitchen.

In spite of these extra comforts the twenty-year-old Princess found her imprisonment very irksome. She was kept confined to her cell for weeks, until she felt ill from lack of air and exercise. She was not allowed to communicate with any of the other prisoners in the Tower, but was told enough about them to dispirit her.

She knew that three rebels, Sir Thomas Wyatt, who had led the Kentish rebellion, Sir James Croft and Edmund Tremayne were being kept alive and horribly tortured in the hope that they might incriminate her. She knew that Archbishop Cranmer, Bishop Ridley and Bishop Latimer were in the Bloody Tower on account of their Protestant beliefs. They would not suffer quickly under the axe but were destined for the slow agony of death by burning at the stake.

Elizabeth herself was subjected to regular cross-examinations by Bishop Gardiner and other members of the Council, who were anxious to find a connection between her and the rebels. On one occasion they even brought Croft to her cell, for he had been to see her before the Rebellion broke out. Gardiner was interested to see her reaction. Elizabeth's response was to say that she had little to say to Croft or "to the rest that were then prisoners in the Tower". She enjoyed a battle of wits and won the admiration of some of the councillors by the way she stood up to cross-examination.

In spite of the tragic associations that the Tower held for her, Elizabeth managed to keep calm, and in time events began to turn in her favour. No damaging evidence could be found against her. Thomas Wyatt was executed on 11 April, and on the scaffold he clearly stated that the Princess had no guilty knowledge of the Rebellion.

At about the same time, she was permitted to take exercise. At first she was only allowed to walk about in the Lieutenant's house, but then she was allowed into his private garden, accompanied always by a strong guard. All other prisoners were forbidden "so much as to look in her direction". Her outings here were brought to an end after she was presented with a posy of flowers by the five-year-old son of the Keeper of the Wardrobe. Posies could contain secret messages, and the garden was declared out of bounds.

Her exercise was now confined to the section of inner wall between the Bell Tower and the Beauchamp Tower. From the ramparts (subsequently known as Princess Elizabeth's Walk) she was greatly heartened by the sights and sounds of normal London life: boys practising archery on Tower Hill; women laying out their washing on the grassy slopes

# The Menagerie

The menagerie at the Tower was started by Henry III with animals presented to him by foreign princes, including an elephant from the King of France. Unfortunately it lived for only a year, but in that time someone drew the elephant and its keeper. Four centuries later James I had the menagerie moved into the Lion Tower where it stayed for the next 200 years.

The menagerie was not a very
well-run place. Sometimes
animals escaped or got into
another cage. Eventually in
1835 William IV ordered the
menagerie to be closed; some
of the animals were sent to the
Zoological Gardens which had
just been opened in Regent's
Park.

of the moat; worshippers entering All Hallows' church; carts rumbling up and down Thames Street; and beyond, the jumbled skyline of church spires, tenements, mansions, and green fields.

On 5 May, Sir John Gage was relieved of his office as Constable, and Sir Henry Bedingfield came into the Tower with a hundred men in blue liveries. Elizabeth feared the worst. She had trusted Gage, but she did not know the new man. She wanted to know if he was the sort of person who "if her murdering was secretly committed to his charge, he would see the execution thereof?" He was not that sort of person. He was a rigid and crusty old gentleman, but he was honest. Besides, he had been given an altogether different task. He had been told to release Elizabeth from the Tower and keep her under house arrest in the manor of Woodstock.

Elizabeth had had a narrow escape which she owed largely to her own cool courage and sagacity. These characteristics stayed with her for the rest of her life, as did her deep dislike of the Tower of London. She never stayed there after her coronation, and allowed the palace buildings to fall into decay.

# 8 Frances Blount and the Martyrs

For Frances Blount, who came to the Tower in 1590, the Tower was never a happy place. She accompanied her father, Sir Michael Blount, who had been made Lieutenant by Elizabeth I. The Queen had not appointed a Constable as superior officer and Sir Michael was in sole charge of the Tower. He was delighted to be following in the footsteps of his father, Sir Richard Blount, who had held the same post twenty-five years earlier.

Prisoners were the Lieutenant's chief responsibility. Fourteen of them were delivered into his custody by his predecessor, Sir Owen Hopton, and by the end of the following year he had acquired several more, including two women. Two warders— Thomas Vannor and Henry Frewen—were in charge of the male prisoners, while Lady Blount and her women saw to the care and locking up of the female prisoners.

Many of the prisoners were in the Tower for their religious beliefs. When she re-established the Church of England at the beginning of her reign, Elizabeth I was anxious to avoid religious persecution, for she had seen the harmful results of Queen Mary's persecution of Protestants. Elizabeth preferred to unite all moderates behind the settlement, but she reckoned without individual religious fervour. Before long, the established Church was being attacked by extreme Protestants at one end, and extreme Catholics at the other.

Blount relished his role as custodian. As a rigid Protestant, he was without sympathy towards those who held differing religious beliefs. He was also attracted by the perquisites of his job. For every prisoner in his care, Blount received a payment from the Exchequer, scaled according to status. In addition, he was allowed a weekly allowance to cover the prisoners' board and that of any servant or gentleman in attendance. Blount soon learnt that if he budgeted carefully he could keep the prisoners for less than the sum allotted for their board, and pocket the difference. He could also lay claim to all the furniture acquired by the prisoners for their rooms when they were released or executed.

Frances felt much more sensitive about the

prisoners than her father did. She could not help feeling sorry for Philip Howard, Earl of Arundel, whom Blount treated with unnecessary severity. Arundel, who had started life as a Protestant, had followed the example of his wife Anne Dacre and become a Catholic convert. So uncompromising was he in his new faith that Elizabeth I imprisoned him in the Tower in 1585. He had been tried for treason and found guilty, but as yet his execution had not been carried out. He was kept a close prisoner in the Beauchamp Tower. There, in his cell on the first floor, he led a monk-like existence with two servants and a dog. He was allowed two hours exercise a day in the company of a warder. The rest of the time he spent praying, fasting and translating religious works.

Frances felt sorrier still for Robert Southwell, the young Jesuit priest who was brought to the Tower in 1592. The Jesuits had formed an underground movement and were infiltrating England with the avowed intention of restoring the Catholic faith and overthrowing the established Protestant religion. The government tracked them down with frightening persistence, and having caught them, put them to torture so as to obtain information and names of accomplices.

Southwell arrived in a dreadful state. He was as thin as a skeleton and was crawling with maggots. He had been caught and horribly mistreated by

Richard Topcliffe, the most notorious of the priest hunters. It was a wonder that Southwell was still alive after his experiences in Topcliffe's private torture chamber, but it was common knowledge that the slender, scholarly priest had revealed nothing under duress.

Blount assigned Southwell to a cell in the Lanthorn Tower where he was kept in solitary confinement according to instructions. He was however allowed a change of clothes, a Bible and the works of St Bernard, which were sent to him by the pious wife of the Earl of Arundel to whom he had been chaplain.

Early in 1594 another Jesuit was brought to the Tower. His name was Henry Walpole and he was put into solitary confinement on the first floor of the Salt Tower. The conditions of his imprisonment were worse than Southwell's. He did not possess enough clothing to keep out the bitter February cold. His bed was a pile of dirty straw and his diet was scanty.

Both priests were put to the torture. This could only be done under special authorization in the name of the Queen because torture was not known to common law. The manacles, by which a prisoner was hung up by the arms, were the fashionable implement of the day. They were just as effective and painful as the rack, but they did less outward damage.

Frances was sickened by the whole business. Unfortunately, she had no one in whom she could confide, for her mother had died in the previous winter. When she voiced her concern to her father, he pointed out that the priests were fortunate not to be in the dungeon among the rats, or the Cell of Little Ease. The first was beneath one of the towers by the river and became infested by rats at high tide. The second was so small that a man could not move or stand upright in it.

The two priests endured their imprisonment with great courage. Southwell made use of his time in confinement to write poems. Before Walpole's fingers were paralysed by torture he scratched his name on the wall of his cell, and on either side of a little oratory he inscribed the names of the orders of the angels, with the names of Mary and Jesus on top. Even Blount, who was a coarse and insensitive man, found himself feeling sorry for them. He took the trouble to inform Walpole's relations that the conditions of his imprisonment were so bad that he "was in need of everything".

Frances was comforted by the thought that although Arundel, Southwell and Walpole never met, they knew of each other's presence in the Tower. All three men had a Norfolk background and their Catholic religion in common. Arundel felt very close to Southwell, for they had corresponded during the time when the priest was chaplain to his wife. The Earl insisted on referring to Southwell as "Blessed Father" although he knew that Blount disapproved. Once when the Lieutenant was visiting the priest, Arundel's dog which had strayed from its quarters came into the cell. When Southwell learned whose dog it was, he gave it his blessing to take back to its master.

The last year Frances spent in the Tower was the worst. During this time she found little to cheer her and much to depress her, including the death of the three men she had come to pity and admire. Southwell was the first to leave the Tower in 1596 for his trial and death. During his trial he stood up for himself with great courage, although the internal injuries he had suffered made it difficult for him to speak. He received the inevitable sentence of death by drawing, hanging and quartering.

Southwell met this terrible death with inspired fortitude. Frances was not present at the scene, but heard all the details later from the Tower Chaplain who was at Tyburn.

As he was dragged on the hurdle from Newgate all the way to Tyburn, Southwell managed to keep his head off the ground so that when the horse drew up at the gallows he was able to get up by himself. He climbed up on to the cart below the noose and addressed some words to those who had come to see him die. He prayed aloud while the hangman arranged the noose round his neck, and was still praying when the cart moved away from him. As he hung by the neck he beat his bound hands against his breast. A sergeant came forward to cut the rope so that the butchering might begin while he was still alive. At this moment there was an unusual interruption: someone stepped forward and waved the sergeant back. When the officers protested, the crowd spontaneously took the side of the priest who was dying so gallantly.

"Let him hang till he be dead," came the cry.

The hangman responded to the appeal and pulled on Southwell's body so that he was spared the sight of his own disembowelling.

Walpole suffered a similar fate in York. The Earl of Arundel would have welcomed a martyr's death, but he died in bed, worn out by years of abstinence and confinement. He petitioned the Queen to allow him to see his wife and child for the last time. Permission was granted on condition that he paid one visit to the established church, a bargain he was not prepared to make. As the Earl grew weaker, Frances noticed that her father was beginning to feel remorseful. At last Blount took himself off to Arundel's bedside and begged his forgiveness. This Arundel freely gave, but could not resist lecturing him on the harsh way he had used his power.

"Remember, good Master Lieutenant," he warned, "that God can in the revolution of a few days bring you to be a prisoner also, and to

# Prisoners in the Tower

The rack and the scavenger's daughter were torture instruments used only at the Tower. The torture was applied gradually. At each stage the prisoner—stretched on the rack or crushed in the scavenger's daughter—would be questioned. If he refused to speak the pain would be made worse. The rack actually had three rollers, not two; the middle one had a locking device to keep the victim stretched out as long as necessary.

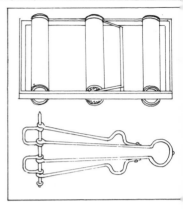

In Elizabeth I's reign many Catholics were imprisoned in the Tower. Some carved inscriptions on the walls of their cells. Some, like the priest Edmund Campion, were hanged, drawn and quartered.

Not all Tower prisoners were there because of religion. Both Lady Catherine Grey (Jane Grey's sister) and Sir Walter Ralegh had displeased the Queen by marrying secretly without her permission.

be kept in the same place where now you keep others."

The extraordinary thing was that Blount fell into disgrace not long afterwards. He was dismissed from his post and confined to the Tower by his successor, and on his release returned to his country seat of Mapledurham in Oxfordshire. Blount bitterly regretted his disgrace and hankered after his lost post, but Frances was only too glad to return to the country. She never wanted to set eyes on the cruel grim fortress again.

# 9 Wat Ralegh and Sir Walter

WHEN SIR WALTER RALEGH was sent to the Tower of London, accompanied by his wife and ten-year-old son Wat, it was not for the first time. Thirteen years earlier, he had been imprisoned for having had the effrontery to marry Bess Throckmorton, one of the Queen's maids-of-honour, without Elizabeth's permission. The Queen had put them both in the Tower, but she was too aware of Ralegh's talents to keep him locked up for long.

This time, however, it was James I who imprisoned Ralegh, and he was ready to keep him in prison indefinitely. Ralegh did not submit meekly to what he considered an unjust imprisonment. He protested that he was innocent of the treason of which he had been convicted, he complained about the conditions of his captivity, and he continually asked to be released. Lady Ralegh made it plain that she felt as outraged as her husband. Young Wat, who was not humble by nature, took his cue from his indomitable parents and held his head high.

The Raleghs moved into the Bloody Tower, which was renovated for them. An upper floor was put in to provide them with extra space, and they set to work to make their rooms as comfortable as possible. They brought in furniture and hung tapestries on the walls. Sir Walter installed himself on the first floor with his two attendants John Talbot and Peter Dean, his magnificent wardrobe and a chestful of books and papers. Lady Ralegh squeezed into the top room with her linen, dresses, female servants and Wat. They were so cramped that the Lieutenant, Sir George Harvey, let Ralegh store his scientific equipment in an old shed in the garden.

Wat and his mother were forced to leave Ralegh for a period when plague broke out in the Tower in the spring of 1604. They moved into a rented house on Tower Hill, and Ralegh, who never missed the chance to complain, wrote a sorrowful letter to the authorities. By the time the plague had disappeared and Wat and Lady Ralegh were able to rejoin Sir Walter in the Tower, there was an addition to the family. The new baby boy was baptised by the name of Carew in the chapel of St Peter ad Vincula on 15 February 1606.

Wat was saved from utter boredom in the Tower by the vitality of his father, who had succeeded in creating a number of interests for himself in captivity. He was growing rare herbs in the Lieutenant's garden, and in his hut he was working on scientific experiments. He made up pills and potions which were in demand from friends and enemies alike. He also manufactured his famous cordial out of bezoar stone, hartshorn, ground pearl, musk, and spirits of wine, with mint, borage, gentian, sugar, sassafras and other herbs.

When Sir William Waad replaced Harvey as Lieutenant, he tried to put the Raleghs in their place. He removed the low wooden fence around the garden and built a high brick wall so that no one could look over. He tightened up the curfews and forbade Lady Ralegh to drive through the gates in her coach. But there was nothing the Lieutenant could do to stop the stream of famous visitors who came to see Ralegh in the Tower, and which even included the Queen and the Prince of Wales.

Queen Anne and Prince Henry took Ralegh's side against the King. Indeed, Henry despised his father for keeping "such a bird in a cage". The Prince was a much more attractive character than his father. James I used to come to the Tower to indulge his love of blood sports, and would spend hours at the pit in the menagerie watching fights between ill-assorted animals. Once he witnessed a lion devouring a live cock after it had refused to touch a lamb. On another occasion he ordered a lion to be set against a bear which had killed a child. When the lion declined to fight, the bear was baited to death by mastiffs.

Henry came to the Tower for quite another reason. He wanted to be educated by one of the best minds in the land. He would ask Ralegh's opinion on all sorts of subjects, from ship-building to marriage, and Ralegh gave his advice freely. He particularly liked to lecture the Prince on the subject of Guiana. Ralegh had been to South America in 1595 and had returned convinced of the existence of a fabulous golden city called Eldorado somewhere in the interior. He was now obsessed with the idea of returning to Guiana to look for the legendary gold mines. But even Prince Henry could not obtain his release, so he settled down to write a History of the World for his royal pupil.

This ambitious project entailed an enormous amount of research. A new supply of books arrived in the Tower, followed by a number of distinguished scholars and the playwright Ben Jonson, who had undertaken to write a chapter. Henry took a close interest in the History and read the pages as they were completed.

In many ways, Ralegh had a more satisfying relationship with the thirteen-year-old Prince than with his own son, who was the same age. Wat

96

had none of Henry's intellectual calibre and could not share to the same extent in his father's cultural and political interests. Wat and his father were also ill-suited temperamentally. Ralegh, who was quick-tempered, was infuriated by Wat's bad-mannered, arrogant, and disrespectful behaviour. The tensions between them were heightened by the close proximity in which they had to live.

The Gunpowder Plot—a Catholic conspiracy to blow up King and Parliament—was of particular interest to the Raleghs, for it brought a fresh batch of prisoners to the Tower. The most notorious of these was Guy Fawkes, who had been caught red-handed in the cellars of the House of Lords. He was interrogated in the Council Chamber in the Lieu-tenant's Lodgings and so severely racked that he could hardly hold his pen to sign his confession. Sir William Waad erected an elaborate plaque in the Chamber to commemorate the discovery of the plot.

Another prisoner indirectly involved in the plot of 1605 was an old friend of Ralegh's—Henry Percy, ninth Earl of Northumberland, nicknamed "the wizard Earl" because of his scientific experiments. His father had been in the Tower before him and had caused a sensation by committing suicide so as to cheat "the bitch" Elizabeth I of his property which would have gone to her upon his convic-tion of treason. As it was, he was able to pass his vast wealth on to his son, who now used some of it to make his prison in the Martin Tower more civilized.

Northumberland paid the Lieutenant £100 for the privilege of not having to eat official prison food. He enlarged the windows in his rooms, laid out paths and a bowling alley in the garden, and built his own still to make spirits. He kept a marvellous library of books on astrology, medicine, navigation, voyages, fortifications and war. He paid three distinguished scholars to keep him company. Thomas Hariot, a brilliant mathematician, Walter Warner and Thomas Hughes were soon known as the "three magi".

The Earl's arrival added a new dimension to the Raleghs' lives in the Tower. Sir Walter was delighted to have the company of someone with as good a mind as his own. The two men with their scholarly cronies created such an intellectual atmosphere in the Tower that it began to feel more like a university than a prison. The Earl, who was stern and moody, preferred not to have his wife with him in prison, but he sometimes sent for his son Lord Percy, who also provided companionship for Wat.

But the Tower was too confined for Wat. By the age of fourteen he was heartily sick of all the petty restrictions. Sir Walter, noting that his well-developed son "liked violent physical exercise and strange company", decided that it was time he went out into the world. Arrangements were made for him to go to Oxford University and then on a foreign tour.

When he returned "home" after behaving very badly abroad, he was astonished to find that his father had become a popular hero to the Londoners who had once hated him. They had come to admire him for his outspoken opposition to the King's policy of appeasement of Spain, which was now generally unpopular. They gathered in crowds to catch a glimpse of him as he walked on the ramparts between the Bloody Tower and the Bell Tower. Much as Ralegh enjoyed his renown, Wat found him sadly changed. Though his mind was still sharp, he had been affected by his long imprisonment. He had suffered at least one stroke and had grown thin and stooped. He had been extremely depressed by the death in 1612 of his patron and admirer Prince Henry. With Henry's death went Ralegh's hopes for release. For a time he even lost interest in his History, but he summoned up his energy and managed to finish it in time for publication in 1614.

James I eventually gave Ralegh his freedom in 1616, but the conditions of his release were deadly. He was to go to Guiana to look for gold, but on pain of death he was not to damage any Spanish property or persons on the way. The dangers inherent in the expedition did not deter Wat. At last he was to do something for which he was suited and he could not wait to set forth in search of the Eldorado of which he had heard so much. He was overjoyed when his father made him captain of the leading ship, the *Destiny*.

Ralegh fell ill on the long and terrible voyage and had to be left behind in Trinidad while a smaller expedition went up the Orinoco. On landing, the expedition clashed with a Spanish settlement. Wat, with his usual impetuosity, had rushed into the attack without thinking. He died fighting gallantly, with a dozen lance wounds in his breast, crying "Go on! Go on!"

When Ralegh received the news of Wat's death, he returned to England a broken man. He was imprisoned in the Tower for the last time, and on 29 October 1618 was executed in front of the Palace of Westminster.

# 10 Elizabeth Edwards and the Crown Jewels

It was after the Restoration of the Monarchy in 1660 that Elizabeth Edwards came to live in the Tower of London. Her father, old Talbot Edwards, was in charge of the coronation regalia, which were now kept at the Tower instead of in Westminster Abbey as formerly. As most of the royal ornaments had been sold or destroyed during the Interregnum, a new set had been especially made for the coronation of Charles II. Only the eagle-shaped ampulla and the anointing spoon dated back to medieval times.

The crowns, sceptres, swords and other treasures were now kept in cupboards on the ground floor of the Martin Tower. Edwards had been given permission by the King to show the regalia to "strangers" and to keep the admission fees in lieu of a salary. He and his family had moved into the top two floors of the Martin Tower.

For some four years Talbot Edwards was able to keep his family in reasonable comfort from the income he earned from the Crown Jewels. In 1665, however, he suffered a sharp business setback when the Plague broke out. The Tower, which had been a popular resort for courtiers and visitors who could afford the thirty-three shillings entrance fee, became deathly quiet. The inmates were forbidden to go outside the walls except on essential errands, and visitors were not allowed in. The fine collection of armour on display became dull and tarnished. The Crown Jewels acquired a layer of dust. Work in the Mint came to a standstill when the Assayer of the Mint, John Woodward, and his watchman were struck down by the disease on the same day.

The three local inns, the King's Head, near the Bell Tower, the Cold Harbour, near the Byward Tower, and the Golden Chain had few customers to serve. Traffic was reduced to the carts which carried out the dead and the sick. Fifty-eight of the garrisoned soldiers, and others suspected of having the disease, were moved to a pest house in Stepney. The Edwards family were among the luckier inhabitants who stayed where they were.

The Plague was hardly over before the Great Fire broke out. The Tower inhabitants first learnt of it on the morning of Sunday 2 September 1666.

Elizabeth hurried up to the roof of the White Tower where a crowd had gathered to watch the fire which was devouring one end of London Bridge. According to the Lieutenant, Sir John Robinson, who was on the roof with his young son, the fire had started in a baker's house in Pudding Lane and had already burnt down most of Fish Street.

To begin with nobody in the Tower felt alarmed, since the fire was still far away and would surely be extinguished before long. But it continued to blaze, destroying everything in its path. By Monday morning the fire was lapping its way northwards along the river bank towards the Tower and there was now a great deal of panic-stricken activity within the walls. What was worrying the inhabitants was the huge store of gunpowder in the White Tower. The fire was so fierce that it was not impossible that it might leap the moat, consume all the wooden shacks and houses that encrusted the outer and inner walls and spread into the Tower itself. If the gunpowder was ignited, the explosion would be horrendous and the damage incalculable.

Meanwhile, hundreds of people were milling around the Tower. Officials kept arriving with the latest news. Carts rumbled in, laden with bullion and treasure rescued from the Goldsmiths' Hall before it was burnt to the ground. The famous diarist Samuel Pepys, who was an official in the Admiralty, kept popping in and out to see what was going on. He had taken the precaution of burying his naval papers, his wine and his parmesan cheese in his garden. People who had lost their homes were seeking refuge in the Tower; others were camping out on the high ground on Tower Hill.

By Tuesday, St Paul's Cathedral was burnt down, the Guildhall was gone, Cheapside was a blackened scar, and the fire had reached Tower Street. The gunpowder had been removed to a safe distance beyond the eastern wall, but the Tower was still in the greatest danger. The decision was taken to blow up the houses in the path of the fire. Explosions were started and the houses on either side of Tower Street collapsed to the ground. The fire, with nothing to feed on, went no further and the Tower was saved.

Life in the Tower gradually returned to normal, but another catastrophe lay in store for the Edwards family, for in 1671 a brazen attempt was made to steal the Crown Jewels. It all started when an ugly parson and his wife came to view the regalia. In fact, the parson was a disreputable Irish adventurer who called himself Colonel Blood, and his "wife" was some accomplice he had picked up in the squalid area around Petty Wales.

Old Talbot Edwards was completely taken in by them, and when the woman pretended to feel faint he called up the stairs to his wife. Mrs Edwards made the woman comfortable, and the parson was most profuse in his thanks. A few days later he returned with the gift of four pairs of gloves and at the same time casually mentioned that he had a handsome and eligible nephew who would make a suitable match for Elizabeth.

Talbot Edwards was delighted with the idea, for Elizabeth was of marriageable age and he was anxious to see her settled before he died. The details were settled at a cosy dinner at which Blood in his guise as a parson said a long grace. He took the precaution of disarming the household by purchasing a case of pistols from them, and arranged to bring the wedding party, nephew included, to the house on the following morning.

Blood and three accomplices arrived deliberately early so as to catch Mrs Edwards and Elizabeth unprepared. Hunt, the so-called nephew and fiancé, was left outside to keep guard. The other two men, Hallowell and Parrot, accompanied Blood into the Martin Tower where they persuaded the poor caretaker to show them the regalia while the women were getting ready upstairs.

As Edwards bent to lock the door behind them the thieves threw a cloak over his head, gagged him and put a clip on his nose to prevent him snorting. Edwards struggled so violently that they eventually hit him on the head with a wooden mallet and brandished a sword before him until he fainted. Parrot stuffed the orb down his baggy breeches,

Blood hid the the crown under his cloak, having first flattened it with a wooden mallet, and Hallowell pocketed the sceptre, which had been filed into sections.

Upstairs, the women were quite oblivious of what was going on below. Elizabeth, who was in a flutter of excitement, had sent her maid to take a peep at her fiancé, but their suspicions had not been roused. As chance would have it, the situation was saved by the unexpected arrival of Elizabeth's brother and a comrade called Captain Beckman. They were surprised to find Hunt outside, but whatever explanation he gave them seemed to satisfy them, for they went on uptstairs.

Hunt rushed into the jewel room to alert his companions. Before they dashed out in panic, Blood plunged his dagger into Edwards who still lay helpless on the floor. The sounds of their departure roused the family at last. When they untied the unfortunate caretaker he could still summon up enough energy to cry, "Treason! The Crown is stolen!" Young Edwards and Beckman immediately took up the cry and set off in pursuit. They saw Blood running ahead, crying "Stop thief!" and pointing in front of him.

Blood fired two shots from his pistol before he was overpowered. During the struggle, some of the precious stones became detached from the crown and rolled into a gutter. Blood seemed unabashed.

"It was a gallant deed, although it failed," he declared. "It was to gain the Crown."

Of the other three, only Hallowell escaped. The stolen treasures were recovered, mended, and restored to the Martin Tower, where for safer keeping they were put behind bars, while a soldier was posted at the entrance. It took rather longer to patch up Talbot's wounds and Elizabeth's self-esteem.

The sequel of the story was curious. Blood was granted a personal audience with Charles II who, amused perhaps at his audacity, or perhaps seeing that Blood could be useful to him as a spy, not only forgave him but rewarded him with a pension and the restoration of some estates in Ireland. Poor Edwards, on the other hand, was only granted a meagre pension after months of petitioning. When he died three years later, his only commemoration was a simple inscription on a stone in St Peter ad Vincula to the effect that he was the late Keeper of his Majesty's Regalia and had died aged eighty years, nine months.

# The Crown Jewels

The coronation of Harold, the last Saxon King of England, in 1066. To this day crown, orb, sceptre and sword are symbols of royalty.

For 300 years every king came to the Tower and, the day before his coronation, rode out in procession through the City of London to Westminster. Here, the boy-King Edward VI, Henry VIII's son, rides beneath a canopy.

After the execution of Charles I the regalia were destroyed, except for the medieval eagle-ampulla and spoon. New regalia had to be made for Charles II.

Saxon and Norman Kings had open crowns. The Tudors had crowns with high arches. Charles II's crowns had depressed arches, like the State Crown used today.

# 11 Mary Sandell and the Mint

MARY SANDELL WAS born, baptised, and brought up in the Tower of London. From 1735 she lived in the Porter's Lodge which was situated at the entrance of the Mint between the outer and inner walls by the Bell Tower. At this time, the Tower was literally bursting at the seams. It was the most overcrowded, busy, dirty place imaginable. A great many officers of the Mint had found the living conditions so intolerable that they had sublet their damp, dilapidated houses and moved out beyond the outer walls.

Mary was glad that her father's job made it impossible for them to leave the Tower, for she found it a most exciting place in which to live.

There was always something going on, and she could never complain of being bored.

As Porter of the Mint, John Sandell was responsible for its security. He had the right to check on everybody who entered or left the premises. He was an industrious man who took his job seriously, with the result that he caught a number of petty thieves red-handed. He also made it his business to track down people who indulged in the crime of "clipping the coin of the Kingdom". When small pieces were cut off coins for the sake of their metal content the coins were not worth their face value. Coin clipping was therefore treated as a crime and a reward of £100 was on constant offer to anyone who gave information leading to the arrest of a culprit. Sandell kept his ear close to the ground, and poked around London so assiduously that he managed to secure the arrest of many such criminals, including a woman called Phebe Carter who subsequently committed suicide in Newgate Gaol. The Treasury recognized his zeal by augmenting his annual salary of £25 by a further £20.

Because of the overcrowding in the Tower, hardly a day passed without some dispute flaring up. The Mint, which occupied the space between the inner and outer walls on the three landward sides of the Tower, was generally at loggerheads with the Board of Ordnance. The Ordnance, which supplied the Army and Navy with artillery, small arms, shot and gunpowder, had expanded into the whole of the White Tower, leaving only St John's Chapel, where the valuable collection of state records was kept. The cellars were crammed with gunpowder, salt-petre and armaments. The site of the old royal palace and the space between the Broad Arrow Tower and the Salt Tower were filled to overflowing with Ordnance offices. The towers along the northern wall which abutted on to the Moneyers Hall and Lodgings were used as factories for the manufacture of firearms. Both Mint and Ordnance, needing to expand, disputed over every inch of ground.

The Mint had to guard its other flank from encroachment by the soldiers. The Regiments from the Royal Fusiliers and the Guards who were in turn garrisoned in the Tower could not always be contained in the insanitary barracks beside the Irish Mint. As likely as not they would then be billeted on the families who lived in the Mint.

There were occasions, such as the birthdays of King George II, when the rival institutions in the Tower were able to sink their differences in common celebrations. The guns were fired from the ramparts, the Warders and gunners shared out twenty-four bottles of wine, and the populace had a jolly time on Tower Hill with a huge bonfire and free barrels of beer. On another memorable occasion everyone stopped work to watch the arrival of a treasure trove. Wagons and wagons of treasure and bullion, captured by two ships in the fleet of Admiral Anson, wound their way up to the Mint in a procession that stretched from the Wharf all the way up to Tower Street.

In 1745, when Mary was ten years old, the peace of more than a decade was rudely disturbed by the Jacobite uprisings in Scotland. The southerners were seized with panic. It was believed that the rebels might reach the capital itself. Lieutenant-General Adam Williamson, the Deputy-Lieutenant of the Tower, who was a staunch Hanoverian, prepared for the worst. He ordered a mountain of extra stores, including bread, brandy, beef, pork, oatmeal, peas, butter, Cheshire cheese and vinegar, to be brought into the Tower in the event of a siege. But the southerners over-estimated the strength of Jacobite support. The Stuart forces were routed, the Young Pretender fled, and in due course a crop of prisoners was brought to the Tower.

Prisoners, trials, and executions were a novelty for Mary, and she was agog with curiosity when the first Highland Lords arrived in 1746. Lord Cromarty was imprisoned in the Bloody Tower, while Lords Balmerino and Kilmarnock were locked up in the Byward Tower. On 24 July 1746 Mary was out on the Parade with the rest of the Tower inmates to see the Lords go to their trial at Westminster. They climbed into separate coaches, and there was a great deal of light-hearted banter about who should ride with the Gentleman Gaoler and the ceremonial axe.

"Come," cried Lord Balmerino, "come put it with me."

The Lords were found guilty. Cromarty was later released, but Kilmarnock and Balmerino went to their executions on 18 August.

Mary and her family had a good view from the outer wall of the Mint. Indeed all the walls and turrets on the westward side of the Tower were filled with spectators. There were even people on top of ships' masts in the river. Others were on the roof of the Transport Office which faced the scaffold, and tier upon tier of spectator stands had been built in the vicinity.

The Sheriffs of London came to the Bulwark Gate to claim the bodies of the victims at ten o'clock in the morning. The prisoners walked in procession with four Warders, the Deputy-Lieutenant, the Tower Major, two chaplains, a few friends, an officer and fifteen soldiers, two hearses with coffins and another detachment of soldiers at the rear.

The scaffold was draped in black, the floor was covered in sawdust and a piece of red baize cloth lay in readiness to receive the heads. Lord Kilmarnock tall and handsome, was the first to be called out. He was visibly taken aback by the number of spectators, but knelt down calmly at the block. His head came off at a stroke, and his body flipped over backwards. Balmerino, who raised his arm when he was ready for death, had his head severed with three strokes.

On 9 April in the following year, Mary witnessed the execution of the last remaining Jacobite leader. The rascally old Lord Lovat, who took a delight in living up to his wild reputation, went to his death almost flippantly. When the Tower Major went to visit him before his execution and asked how he was, Lovat replied,

"I am doing very well, for I am preparing myself for a place where hardly any Majors and very few Lieutenant-Generals go."

Lovat was so infirm and bloated that he had to be taken to the Transport Office by coach. When he stepped on to the scaffold he was amazed to see how many people had come out to see "the taking off of an old grey head". He remarked that they were all piled up "like rotten oranges". He would have been amused to hear that there had been an accident earlier in the day, when one of the stands had collapsed. He then drank a bumper to King James and declared that "if I had a thousand lives, I would lay them all down here in the same cause." He presented the executioner John Thrift with ten guineas, and instructed him,

"Pray do your work well; for if you should cut

# The Mint

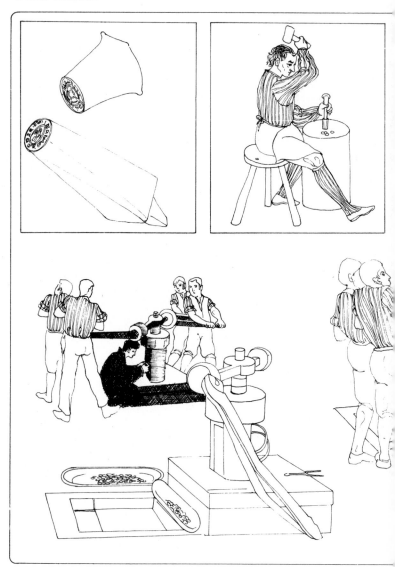

Coins were struck by hand until 1662, when the coining press was introduced. The upper die was brought down on to a metal blank, which had been placed on top of the lower die, by four men turning a large screw; another man fed the blanks into the press. This method was used until the Mint left the Tower in 1811, after which steam-power was used.

The coin at the top is an Edward III silver groat. The coin in the middle is a Charles II guinea, made of gold from West Africa, which was then called Guinea. The coin at the bottom is a George III silver shilling.

and hack my shoulders and I shall be able to rise again, I shall be angry."

Although Mary lived in the Tower until she died in 1763, Lovat's was the last execution she ever saw, for he happened to be the last noble prisoner to be beheaded on Tower Hill.

# 12 William Kinch and the Fire of 1841

WILLIAM KINCH LIVED in the Tower of London
during the period of reforms brought about by the
Duke of Wellington, who had been appointed
Constable in 1826. Although the Duke was fifty-
seven years old, and had all his legendary military
exploits behind him, he was not one to rest on his
laurels. He had very definite ideas about the Tower
of London and took his job seriously.

William's father, George Kinch, owed his appointment as Yeoman Warder in 1832 directly to the
Duke, for one of his first reforms had been to change
the rules regarding the appointment of Yeoman
Warders. When the posts fell vacant, they could no
longer be bought and sold as in former times, but
were given instead to retired soldiers with records of

gallantry. George Kinch had been a Sergeant in the Light Dragoons for twenty-five years. After the change, the Warders (who still dressed in the Tudor costume of their predecessors) remembered the old custom of purchase in the ancient toast they drank to one another, "May you never die a Warder". When a Warder died in the old days it was the Constable who received the fees from his successor.

The Duke, with his hooked nose and erect carriage, was a familiar figure in the Tower while William was growing up. He paid frequent visits, and no detail was too small for his attention. For instance, he disapproved of the way some of the inmates took advantage of the privileges they enjoyed because they lived within the "Liberties of the Tower". Because no bailiffs were allowed into the Tower many people were neglecting to pay their debts.

The Duke looked upon the Tower primarily as a fortress. This was a somewhat old-fashioned view to hold, but he was obsessed by the memory of the French Revolution and feared similar outbreaks of mob violence in London. He was therefore deeply concerned by the decay into which the Tower had fallen. The Lanthorn Tower was a burnt ruin, sections of the walls were crumbling, and the chapel of St Peter ad Vincula was in disrepair. The moat was a stinking, stagnant cesspool which had more than once caused cholera among the thousand or so inhabitants of the Tower and the people who lived outside the walls.

Many of the repairs proposed by the Duke were ruled out by the government on the grounds of expense, but he did succeed in getting a bastion built into the northern wall, and he made a real attempt to clean up the moat. First he had some of the filth removed in barges at a cost of £1,000, then he ordered it to be regularly flooded, dammed and stirred about. Unfortunately the smell caused by the process of cleaning was appalling and when there was another outbreak of cholera the residents in St Katharine's Dock decided it was the stench that had caused the disease. They petitioned for the "Scraping Process" to stop, and Wellington was forced to comply.

The Duke was very uneasy about the crowds of visitors who came to see the sights at the Tower. He looked upon them as a threat to the security of his fortress and feared that they could get out of control at any moment. But people had been coming to see the Tower for centuries, and even the Duke could not put an end to the custom now.

There was not so much to see as formerly, for the menagerie had recently been moved out of the Tower. Under a remarkable Keeper by the name of Alfred Cops it had acquired a baboon, a kangaroo, monkeys, alligators, snakes and a secretary bird. Not very surprisingly such overcrowding led to a number of nasty accidents. The secretary bird had its head bitten off by a hyena and Mr Cops himself was almost throttled by a boa-constrictor. After an officer and a soldier had been bitten by a lion, the zoo was ordered to be disbanded, by royal command. For a long time afterwards touts outside the gates went on selling tickets to the more gullible for a "Lion Washing Ceremony". The only creatures left were the black ravens. They had acquired a more permanent dwelling in the boiler house, which had once been the cowbyre in the Lieutenant's Lodgings.

The Mint had also gone to more spacious premises on Tower Hill, so that the chief attractions now remaining were the Crown Jewels and the collections of arms and armour. After Queen Victoria's coronation, so many visitors had come to see the Crown Jewels that it had been necessary to assign an extra number of Warders to guide duties. The entrance fee to the Tower was now five shillings. Two shillings of this went to the Treasurer of the Ordnance, two shillings to the Keeper of the Crown Jewels, and one shilling to the Warder in attendance.

Almost as popular with visitors were the arms and armour, which were housed in six armouries altogether. The Spanish Armoury near the White Tower contained weapons supposedly captured from the Spanish Armada. The famous "Line of Kings"—a series of mounted figures in armour—

had recently been reorganized by Sir Samuel Meyrick, the Keeper of the Armouries, who had discovered such terrible errors as the Conqueror in plate armour, and George II in a decorated suit of seventeenth-century armour. Having rearranged the armour, he had it rehoused in the New Horse Armoury to the south of the White Tower. In the Grand Storehouse which had been completed in the reign of William and Mary, there was a collection of small arms arranged into fantastic shapes such as Medusa's head, and the waves of the sea.

Unfortunately, all these small arms, together with a valuable collection of battle trophies, stands of service weapons and a quantity of ammunition, were destroyed in the Great Fire of 1841, when William Kinch was eleven. When the curfew bell rang out in warning on that fateful night, the Kinch family rushed outside to see what was going on. The Grand Storehouse was consumed with flames. The Tower of London was in the greatest jeopardy, for the vaults of the Storehouse were crammed with rounds of ball cartridges and barrels of gunpowder. The White Tower to the south contained another stock of gunpowder.

Major Elrington, the Tower Major, immediately mounted a fire-fighting operation. He had the soldiers of the Scots Fusilier Guards and the Royal Artillery, who were on garrison duty, to help him, as well as the Yeomen Warders. The gates were shut so that no one could enter or leave the Tower without permission. The borough fire engines which had come promptly to the scene were dragged into position and connected to pumping engines on the Wharf.

The Scots Fusilier Guards tackled the Grand Storehouse itself. Finding that they could not enter by the door, they climbed in through a window. By forming a line and passing objects from one to another they were able to save a few valuable armaments before the roof crashed in. Meanwhile, the soldiers of the Royal Artillery were working at top speed to remove the powder from the White Tower. Some Warders were up on the roof sweeping off burning embers and laying wet blankets over the skylights, while hoses were kept in play on the walls.

The noise and confusion were horrific. The flames crackled and roared, and were reflected in the sky by an orange patch that could be seen for miles. People wailed and shouted and cursed, while the bell on top of the Bell Tower rang and rang. From the river came the sound of firemen's gongs, and explosions split the air as gunpowder or buildings were deliberately destroyed.

When the fire was at its height, a decision was made to save the Crown Jewels from the Martin Tower which was so close to the burning Storehouse. During the rescue operation there were some differences of opinion between Colonel Eden, who was the officer in command of the Scots Fusilier Guards, and Mr Swifte, the Keeper of the Jewel House. At one point Mrs Swifte declined to lend Eden her shawl to cover the famous State Salt modelled on Exeter Castle, and one of the soldiers had to provide a scarf instead.

Nevertheless, between them all, the precious jewels were eventually saved. The protective iron grille had to be forced with crowbars before the regalia could be taken to safety. Colonel Eden kept a note of each item, together with the name of the person who carried it to the Queen's House. George Kinch was noted down on the list for carrying two salts with lids on one trip, and spurs and bracelets and another salt on a second trip.

By 2 a.m. the fire was under control. By 6 a.m. it was possible to inspect the damage. The roofless Storehouse was a terrible sight—a charred skeleton streaked with molten lead from the roof. The interior was nothing but a jumble of twisted metal. The Bowyer Tower was also badly damaged. This Tower had been used for cleaning and mending armaments, and it was here, from an overheated oven, that the fire started. The Brick Tower next door to it was partially burnt, while the cloth upon which the Crown Jewels had lain was found to be charred.

By the following morning, even fashionable

ladies could be seen picking over the smouldering ruins in search of souvenirs. The Duke of Wellington himself came to inspect the damage. With characteristic energy and determination, he resolved to start a programme of improvements and restoration which had long been overdue. As usual, he made the military his first consideration. He had a huge barracks built for his beloved soldiers on the site of the Grand Storehouse, and he himself laid the foundation stone.

Soon the Tower was humming with activity. Workmen were everywhere, pulling down old buildings and putting up new ones. The shacks and houses which had cluttered up the site of the old palace and the space between the walls were completely destroyed. Along with them went the Tower's last remaining tavern, the Golden Chain. The Kinchs' house on the Parade was pulled down, and they had to be rehoused.

The Warders were inclined to think the changes too drastic. They were sorry to see the destruction of so many historic landmarks, and they deeply resented the favouritism shown to the garrisoned soldiers, whom they had always regarded as less important than themselves. William, however, enjoyed the restoration work. When at last the moat was drained, he was there to watch as from the sediment of ages an interesting collection of objects was unearthed. There were Roman coins, human and animal bones, large cannon balls which experts dated to the Wars of the Roses, Tudor bottles and countless other relics. William saw laid out before his eyes a tiny part of the Tower's long and fascinating history.

# Tower Ceremonies

The most famous of all Tower ceremonies is the Keys, which is carried out every night. The Chief Yeoman Warder locks the gates at the main entrance and under the Middle Tower and the Byward Tower.

At the Bloody Tower the Chief Warder and his escort are challenged by the sentry:
"Halt, who goes there?"
"The keys."
"Whose keys?"
"Queen Elizabeth's keys."

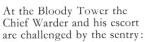

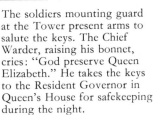

The soldiers mounting guard at the Tower present arms to salute the keys. The Chief Warder, raising his bonnet, cries: "God preserve Queen Elizabeth." He takes the keys to the Resident Governor in Queen's House for safekeeping during the night.

On state occasions the Yeoman Warders wear their scarlet and gold ceremonial uniforms in Tudor style. On parade the Yeoman Gaoler carries the ceremonial axe and the Chief Warder the mace (the head is a miniature replica of the White Tower).

Every third year the Chief Warder and the Chaplain lead the Tower children and local choirboys in a procession from St Peter's Chapel to each of the boundary stones that mark the parish of the Tower, and the children "beat the bounds".

Royal salutes of 62 guns are fired on State occasions from the Tower Wharf by the Honourable Artillery Company.

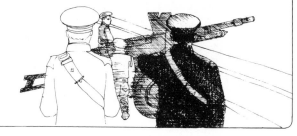

# Epilogue:
# The Tower Today

TODAY THE TOWER OF LONDON is visited each year by more than two million tourists, who want to see for themselves Britain's most famous historic monument. The Tower's development as a military fortress is obvious at a glance. The White Tower is still the dominating feature. All but a few of the original arrow slits have been replaced by classical windows, but the wooden staircase leading directly to the first floor has been reconstructed. The inner and outer defensive walls, punctuated by towers, have not changed radically since the time of Edward I. The moat has been grassed over but its course is clearly visible. Although the Bulwark Gate, the Lion Tower and the drawbridges have gone from the western entrance, it is easy to work out the general layout of Edward I's fortified gateway. And in the Byward Tower (largely unchanged since the thirteenth century) a portcullis is still in position, complete with its working machinery. The river no longer flows under the Traitors' Gate, but the archway with its enormous span remains an awesome sight.

The Tower's function as a prison is also self-evident. The Bloody Tower, which tradition has associated with the murder of the little princes, and where the Raleghs were cooped up for so long, is open to the public. The inscriptions preserved in the Beauchamp Tower are a vivid reminder of the agony of some of its inmates. The Earl of Arundel left his mark in a careful Latin inscription, which translated reads, "By so much the more affliction for Christ in this world, so much the more glory with Christ in the future." The block and axe used for the execution of Lord Lovat can be seen in the Bowyer Tower. The spot on Tower Green where three Queens perished is marked by a plaque. Close by is the chapel of St Peter ad Vincula which is so full of headless bodies that the historian Macaulay called it "the saddest spot on earth".

In contrast with this dark side, the sunny side of the Tower must now be left largely to the imagination. The palace buildings which Henry and Eleanor of Provence embellished so lavishly have disappeared. Some beautiful wall decorations have been uncovered in the Byward Tower, but these were painted in the reign of Richard II. When the Mint, menagerie, records and arsenal left the Tower, a working population of ordinary citizens went with them. Now only fifty or so families live within the precincts, includng the Resident Governor who occupies the Queen's House (formerly the Lieutenant's Lodgings).

Garrisoned soldiers have a continuing role in the Tower. The Household Division send detachments to the Tower for twenty-four or forty-eight hour duties. The Royal Fusiliers have made the Tower their regimental headquarters and have an Officers' Mess and a Museum at their disposal. The royal salutes from the guns on the Wharf are now fired by the Honourable Artillery Company, who took up this duty at the Tower in 1924.

Some of the ancient ceremonials associated with the Tower have died. Charles II was the last King to process from the Tower to Westminster before his coronation, accompanied by the Knights of the Bath who, by ancient tradition, had received their knighthoods beforehand at the Tower. But there are plenty of ceremonies which have survived unchanged, such as the Beating of the Bounds on Ascension Day, the Parade of the Yeoman Warders at Christmas, Easter and Whitsun and the Ceremony of the Keys. Once a year on 21 May, the Provosts of Eton and King's College, Cambridge bring white lilies and roses to lay in the oratory in the Wakefield Tower in memory of Henry VI.

The ravens who have been part of the scene from the beginning have become a legend in themselves. It is said that if the ravens were to leave, the Tower would fall. They live in style under the care of a Yeoman Warder who has the title of Raven Master. They have a roomy cage and are fed on a diet of lean meat, raw egg and biscuit. If one of the resident ravens dies it is at once replaced by another.

One suspects that the ravens are on to a good thing. Is it not fanciful to suppose that the Tower, which has survived as a symbol of power and endurance through times of civil strife and neglect, would crumble at the desertion of a handful of birds?

# Index